NO GALLBLAD COOKBOOK

1000 days Mouthwatering Recipes | Ultimate Diet Guide for Health and Wellness after Gallbladder Removal Surgery | Pain Relief Cookbook for Gallbladder Disorder

TYLER RUIZ

TABLE OF CONTENTS

INTRODUCTION

The gallbladder stores and excretes bile. Bile is a specific fluid produced by the liver that aids in the digestion of fats in your diet.

The gallbladder is located in the upper right of your abdomen (belly). It sits just under your liver.

It is a component of your digestive system. Its primary role is to hold bile. Bile aids your digestive system in the breakdown of fats. Bile is mainly composed of cholesterol, bilirubin, and bile salts.

The biliary tract connects your gallbladder to the rest of your digestive system via bile ducts. The biliary tract is a pipe-like system that transports bile from the liver to the small intestine.

It is a component of your digestive system, and its primary role is to hold bile. Bile aids your digestive system in the breakdown of fats, and bitterness is mainly composed of cholesterol, bilirubin, and bile salts.

The biliary tract connects your gallbladder to the rest of your digestive system via bile ducts.

CHAPTER 1
GUIDE TO GALLSTONES

The gallbladder is a pouch holding bile, a green-yellow liquid that aids digestion. Gallbladder problems often occur when something like a gallstone blocks the bile duct.

Most gallstones are created when substances found in bile, like cholesterol, harden.

Gallstones are very common and routinely asymptomatic. However, approximately 10% of patients diagnosed with gallstones will have symptoms within five years.

Gallstone signs and symptoms

Gallstones might cause pain in your upper right abdomen or stomach area. Gallbladder discomfort may occasionally occur after eating high-fat foods, such as fried dishes, but it can happen anytime. Gallstone pain typically lasts only a few hours, although it can be excruciating.

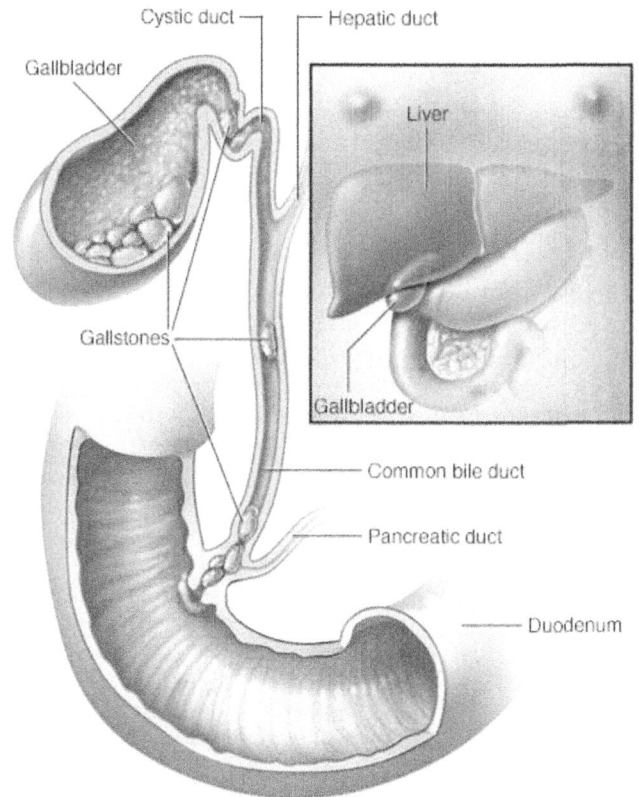

If gallstones are not treated or discovered, the following symptoms may develop:

- a fast heartbeat caused by a high temperature

- skin yellowing and whites of the eyes (jaundice)

- diarrhea, cold, and confusion

- a decrease in appetite

- Gallbladder infection or inflammation of the liver or pancreas can cause these symptoms.

Gallstones with no symptoms

Gallstones do not produce pain on their own. Pain develops when gallstones obstruct bile movement from the gallbladder.

According to the American College of Gastroenterology, "silent gallstones" affect approximately 80% of persons with gallstones. This indicates they are free of discomfort and symptoms. In these circumstances, your doctor may uncover gallstones via X-rays or during abdominal surgery.

Causes

Gallstones are thought to be caused by a chemical imbalance of bile within the gallbladder. While experts are yet unsure what causes the imbalance, there are a few probable explanations:

There is too much cholesterol.

A buildup of cholesterol in your bile might result in yellow cholesterol stones. Hard stones can form if your liver produces more cholesterol than your bile can break down.

There is much bilirubin in your bile.

Bilirubin is a substance created naturally during the breakdown of red blood cells. It is produced, passed via the liver, and subsequently eliminated from the body.

Some medical diseases, such as liver damage and blood disorders, lead your liver to produce more bilirubin than it should. When the gallbladder cannot break down excess bilirubin, pigment gallstones form. These rough stones are frequently dark brown or black.

Bile that has been concentrated due to a full gallbladder

To function effectively, your gallbladder must be able to empty its bile. If it does not open its bile content, the bitterness gets too concentrated, which can lead to the formation of stones.

Treatment

Most of the time, you won't need gallstone therapy until they cause you discomfort. Gallstones can travel through your body without your knowledge. If you are in agony, your doctor will most likely advise you to get surgery. Medication may be utilized in rare circumstances.

If you are at high risk of surgical complications, there are a few nonsurgical options for treating gallstones. However, your gallstones may return with continued treatment if surgery is not performed, implying you may need to monitor your condition for the rest of your life.

Surgery

Cholecystectomy, or gallbladder surgery, is one of the most common operations performed on adults in the United States. Because the gallbladder isn't a vital organ, you can live a healthy life without it.

Cholecystectomy comes in two varieties:

Cholecystectomy is performed laparoscopically. This is a standard procedure that necessitates general anesthesia. In most cases, the surgeon will make three or four incisions in your belly. They'll delicately remove your gallbladder after inserting a small, illuminated gadget into one of the incisions. If there are no issues, you can generally go home the same day or the next day.

Cholecystectomy with an open incision. This procedure is usually performed when the gallbladder is inflamed, diseased, or scarred. This operation may also be performed if complications arise during laparoscopic cholecystectomy.

Stools may be loose or watery after gallbladder ectomy. When a gallbladder is removed, the bile must be redirected from the liver to the small intestine. Since the gallbladder is no longer in use, bile is diluted. The initial consequence is a laxative effect that can produce diarrhea, but for most people, this will resolve on its own.

Nonsurgical therapies

If surgery is not an option, such as if the patient is very old, doctors can try a few additional methods to remove the gallstones.

Oral dissolving therapy combines the medicines ursodiol (Actigall) and chenodiol (Chenix) to break up gallstones. These drugs contain bile acids, which help to dissolve the stones. This procedure is ideal for breaking up cholesterol stones and can take months or years to work fully.

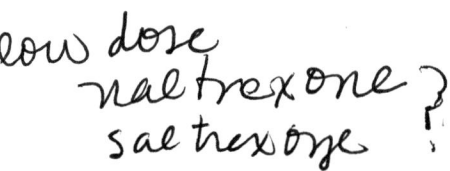

low dose
naltrexone?
saltrexone?

Another alternative is shock wave lithotripsy. A lithotripter is a machine that sends shock waves through a person's body. These shock waves can shatter gallstones into smaller pieces.

Percutaneous gallbladder drainage is performed by inserting a sterile needle into the gallbladder and aspirating (drawing out) bile. A tube is then placed to aid in further drainage. This operation isn't usually the first line of defense and is generally reserved for people who aren't candidates for other procedures.

Gallstone risk factors

Some gallstone risk factors are nutrition-related, whereas others are not as easily controlled. All uncontrollable risk factors are age, color, gender, and family history.

Risk factors in one's lifestyle

- Obesity diets are heavy in fat or cholesterol and lacking in fiber

- going through a quick weight loss

- having type 2 diabetes

- Factors of genetic risk

- being a woman of Native American or Mexican descent

- being 60+ years or more, having a family history of gallstones

- Medical danger signs

- surviving cirrhosis

- being pregnant and taking cholesterol-lowering drugs

- taking estrogen-containing medicines (like specific birth control)

While some medications may raise your risk of gallstones, don't stop taking them unless you've discussed them with your doctor and received their clearance.

Diagnosis

Your doctor will examine you physically, including assessing your eyes and skin for noticeable color changes. A yellowish tinge may indicate jaundice caused by excess bilirubin in your body.

Different tests that allow your doctor to look inside your body may be used during the checkup. Among these tests are:

Ultrasound. Your abdomen is imaged with an ultrasound. It is the preferred imaging approach for confirming gallstone disease. It may also reveal anomalies related to acute cholecystitis.

CT scan of the abdomen. This imaging examination photographs your liver and abdominal region.

Radionuclide scan of the gallbladder. This vital scan takes approximately one hour to complete. Radioactive material is injected into your veins by a professional. This chemical enters your bloodstream and travels to your liver and gallbladder. A scan may reveal indications of illness or bile duct blockage caused by stones.

Blood tests are performed. Your doctor might prescribe a blood test to check your bilirubin levels if they are concerned about you. Your liver's health and functionality can be determined by the tests as well.

CHAPTER 2

MODERATE DIET AND FOODS TO CONSUME

Try the following tips to assist improve your condition and lower your chance of gallstones:

- Consume fewer processed carbohydrates (such as cookies and white bread) and less sugar.

- Increase your diet of good fats, such as fish oil and olive oil, which may aid in the contraction and emptying of your gallbladder.

- Consume a limited amount of fiber daily (women need about 25 grams daily, and men need about 38 grams daily).

- Every day, engage in some form of physical activity.

- Maintain proper hydration.

- Lose weight gradually if you want to. Rapid weight loss may raise your chances of developing gallstones and other health issues.

Prevention

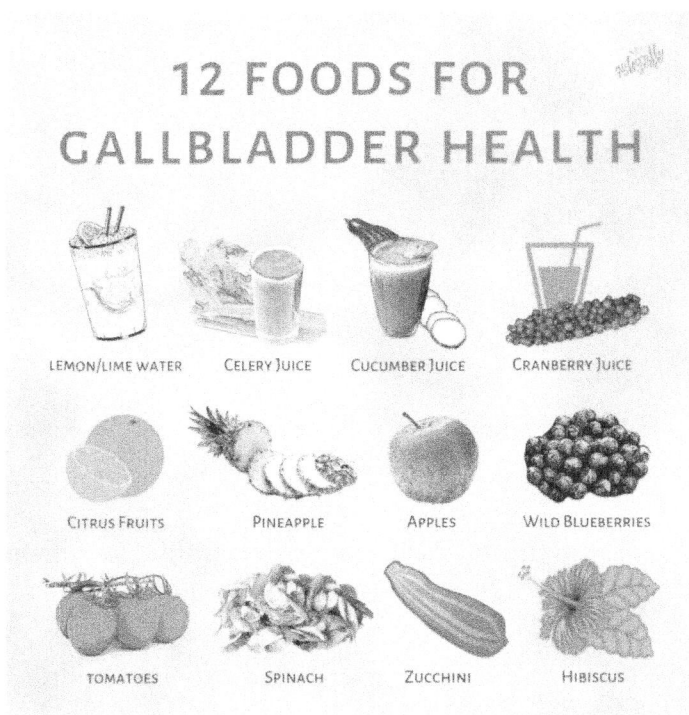

While there is no failsafe technique to prevent gallstones entirely, cholesterol does play a significant part in their production. You should reduce your intake of foods high in saturated fat. Among these meals are fatty meats such as sausage and bacon, cakes and cookies, lard and cream, and some cheeses.

Dietary Guidelines for a Healthy Gallbladder

Gallstones and cancer are two gallbladder disorders that can be avoided with dietary changes.

According to research, persons who eat a healthy diet have a lower chance of gallbladder disease.

Knowing which foods to eat and which to avoid can help the gallbladder stay healthy, especially for people who have gallstones or other gallbladder problems.

Although there is no recommended diet for a healthy gallbladder, following a few tips will help maintain the gallbladder healthy and operating correctly.

Foods to consume

The gallbladder diet seeks to alleviate the stress that diet can place on the gallbladder by simplifying digestion or supporting the gallbladder. A 2015 study looked at 114 ladies' food patterns and risk of gallstones.

The researchers defined two types of diets for this study:

Fresh fruits and green vegetables, fruit juice, low-fat dairy products, whole grains, nuts, spices, and legumes are all part of a healthy diet.

A diet high in processed meat, soft drinks, refined grains, red meat, high-fat products, high sugar, tea, fat, baked potato, snacks, egg, too much salt, pickled food, and sauerkraut is unhealthy.

People who ate a well-balanced diet were less likely to develop gallbladder disease.

Here are some specific foods to avoid to keep your gallbladder healthy.

Foods derived from plants

A nutritious diet will provide a wide range of nutrients. A diet rich in plant foods can supply the nutrients the body requires to stay healthy.

Vitamins, minerals, and antioxidants are abundant in plant-based meals. These may aid in the prevention of gallbladder disease.

Antioxidants are nutrients that aid in removing harmful chemicals known as free radicals from the body.

Lean protein

Protein is required for bodily tissue repair and growth. Red meat and dairy products are abundant in protein but also heavy in fat, which can stress the gallbladder.

Low-fat protein dishes are an excellent choice. They include:

- Poultry

- Fish

- Low-fat items made from milk

- seeds and nuts

- soy and soy-related items

- legumes like beans and lentils

- Soy milk, for example, is a dairy substitute.

Added salt is commonly found in processed meats and dairy products. Fresh foods with no added sugar are a healthier option.

A 2016 study discovered a relationship between a high vegetable protein diet and a lower risk of gallbladder disease.

Fiber

Fiber, according to experts, promotes digestive health and may protect against gallbladder disease by increasing the passage of food through the stomach and decreasing the generation of secondary bile acids.

In 2014, researchers investigated how a high-fiber diet affects biliary sludge production during a quick weight-loss diet for obese patients. Biliary or gallbladder sludge is a material that increases the likelihood of gallbladder disease developing. It can accumulate in persons who fast or lose weight rapidly.

Those who ate a high-fiber diet developed less gallbladder sludge, lowering their risk of gallbladder disease. This shows that fiber may aid in preventing gallbladder disease in persons who need to reduce weight quickly and possibly permanently. Fruits, green vegetables, legumes, nuts, and seeds are all good sources of fiber:

- Complete grains

- Healthy fats

- Unsaturated fats, such as omega-3, may aid in gallbladder protection.

- Cold-water fish, dry fruits, nuts, walnuts, and seeds such as flaxseeds.

People can also take different supplements, but they should consult a doctor first because some accessories are inappropriate for everyone.

Coffee

Coffee used in moderation may help safeguard gallbladder function. According to research, several compounds in coffee may have varied effects on gallbladder function, including balancing specific chemicals and boosting gallbladder and perhaps intestine activity.

Calcium

A sufficient calcium intake in the diet can benefit gallbladder health. Calcium can be found in dark, leafy greens like kale and broccoli. Dairy products, including yogurt, cheese, and milk dairy substitutes, added nutrients, such as almond or flax milk, sardine and the juice of oranges. People who are predisposed to gallbladder disease should consume zero-fat dairy products.

Folate, magnesium, and vitamin C

Vitamin C, magnesium, and folate may all aid in the prevention of gallbladder disease:

- Citrus fruits and vegetables

- kiwifruit

- broccoli

- strawberries

- tomatoes

Because vitamin C is a water-soluble vitamin, boiling in water may remove some of it from the meal. The most excellent sources are fresh, uncooked fruits and vegetables.

- Almonds and cashews contain magnesium.

- peanut butter and peanuts

- spinach beans, black beans, and edamame

- milk made from soy

- potato

- avocado

- rice

- yogurt

- banana

- Beef liver and spinach are high in folate.

- cereals enriched with black-eyed peas

- asparagus

Although supplements are available, obtaining nutrients from the diet is preferable. Before taking supplements, people should consult with their doctor.

Avoidance foods

Some foods may raise the risk of gallbladder problems like gallstones. Those who are concerned about the health of their gallbladder should avoid or limit the foods listed below.

Carbohydrate refinement

Carbohydrates are vital components in most people's diets, and unrefined carbohydrates, such as whole grains and oats, can give them.

Refined carbs, on the other hand, may raise the risk of gallbladder diseases. According to one study, eating 40 grams (g) or more of sugar per day quadrupled the incidence of gallstones with symptoms.

- Added sugars and sweeteners are carbs to limit or avoid.

- blanched flour

- different refined grains

- ready-made baked items, such as cookies and cakes

- chocolate and candy

Fats that are unhealthy

The gallbladder generates bile, which aids the body's digestion of lipids. A high-fat diet, particularly saturated and trans fats, may burden this mechanism more.

Researchers discovered that those who consume red, processed meats and eggs as part of an unhealthy diet are more likely to develop gallstones.

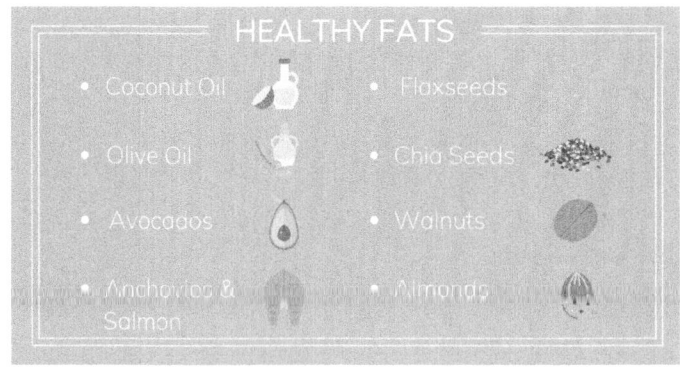

Unhealthy fats can be found in:

- red, fatty meats

- prepared meats

- other prepared foods

- dairy products with total fat

- foods that are fried

- numerous fast foods

- salad dressings and sauces already made

- baked goods and desserts already made

- chocolate and other sweets

- frozen yogurt

Following gallbladder removal

People who have gallbladder surgery can digest food, but they may need to make some dietary changes for a few days or weeks. A doctor may advise a patient to eat small meals in the days following surgery. For several weeks, adhere to a low-fat diet. If the person has bloating, diarrhea, or other digestive symptoms, it may be beneficial to avoid caffeine.

Avoid foods that are spicy or fatty.

Avoid anything that aggravates your symptoms. Gradually increase the amount of organic fiber in your diet

Anyone who notices greasy or foamy stools should seek medical attention. A gallbladder cleanses, flushing or detox is a dietary trend that scientists have labeled "misleading."

According to proponents, it can reset the gallbladder, flush out gallstones, improve digestive health, and improve gallbladder function. For two weeks, consume a rigorous diet with apple juice, followed by Epsom salts and a blend of olive oil and citrus juice.

Experts warn that recommending this diet without sufficient evidence is risky. Many people claim to notice "stones" in their feces; however, the scientific examination has shown that they are clumps of oil and citrus juice. Anyone concerned about gallbladder disease should consult a physician.

CHAPTER 3

SIMPLE AND DELICIOUS NO-GALLBLADDER RECIPES

Strawberry French Toast Casserole

Cook Time: 50 minutes

Servings: 8

Ingredients:

- Eight pieces spelled flour bread, chopped
- 1 1/2 cups strawberries, chopped
- 2 1/4 cups almond milk
- 1/4 cup almond butter
- 1/4 teaspoon salt
- 1/3 cup agave syrup
- Two tablespoons of ground flax meal

Instructions:

1. Preheat your oven to 350.0 F, and grease a baking dish with cooking spray. Add bread and strawberries to it.
2. Mix milk, butter, syrup, and salt in a bowl. Pour over the bread and berries mixture and let rest for 30 minutes.
3. Bake for 45-50 minutes. Let cool slightly and serve.

Nutritional information: 200 calories; 6 g fat; 30 g total carbs; 8 g protein

Quick Vegan Breakfast Burritos

Cook Time: 30 minutes

Servings: 2 burritos

Ingredients:

- 1 1/2 cups water
- 3/4 cup quinoa, cooked
- 1/4 cup cilantro, chopped
- 1/2 teaspoon salt
- 1/2 onion
- One squash, cubed
- Two tablespoons of almond butter
- 1/4 teaspoon black pepper
- 1 cup garbanzo beans, cooked
- 1/4 teaspoon chili, cumin, and garlic powder
- 1/4 avocado
- Greens
- Two spelt spelled flour tortillas
- 1/4 cup organic salsa

Instructions:

1. Cut onion into 1/4" rings. Heat a skillet over medium heat. Add vegan butter and coat. Add squash to one side and onions to the other. Season and cover, and cook for 5 minutes on one side and 5 minutes on the other. Remove and set aside.

2. Add beans to a pan placed over medium heat and season with garlic powder, cumin, and chili powder. Once bubbles form, reduce heat.

3. Mix avocado and greens in a bowl. Season and set coleslaw aside. Add cilantro to quinoa and toss.

4. Add fillings, avocado, and salsa. Roll into burritos, slice, and serve.

Nutritional information (per serving): 285 calories; 17 g fat; 1 g total carbs; 30 g protein

Alkaline Omelet

Cook Time: 5 minutes

Servings: 1

Ingredients:

- 1/4 cup garbanzo bean flour
- 1/3 cup water
- 1/4 teaspoon sweet basil
- 1/4 teaspoon onion powder
- 1/4 teaspoon sea salt
- 1/4 teaspoon oregano
- 1/4 teaspoon cayenne powder
- 1/4 cup Roma tomato, diced
- 1/4 cup onion, chopped
- 1/4 cup bell pepper, diced
- 1/4 cup mushrooms, chopped
- Grapeseed Oil

Instructions:

1. Mix water and flour in a bowl, add all seasonings and stir well.
2. Add oil to the skillet and preheat over medium heat. Add all vegetables and cook for 3-4 minutes.
3. Add flour mixture and cook for 3-4 minutes. Flip it and cook for a few minutes more. Enjoy!

Nutritional information (per serving): 235 calories; 13 g fat; 10 g total carbs; 20 g protein

Banana-Ginger Pancakes

Cook Time: 6 minutes

Servings: 4

Ingredients:

- One ¼ cups almond milk
- One ¼ cup spelled flour _spelt_
- 1 ½ teaspoons ground ginger
- Two teaspoons of baking powder
- Two tablespoons of agave nectar
- One teaspoon of vanilla extract
- Two tablespoons of applesauce, unsweetened
- 1 cup mashed bananas
- ¼ teaspoon salt
- vegetable oil

Instructions:

1. Mix baking powder, flour, ginger, and salt in a bowl.
2. Mix soy milk, agave nectar, vanilla, and applesauce in another bowl.
3. Add
4. bananas.

17

5. Heat a small-sized skillet over medium heat and coat it with oil. Add ¼ cup batter to the skillet. Flip the pancake when tiny bubbles appear on top. Flip the pancake and cook for 2 minutes. Cook pancakes for 2 minutes per side.

6. Once done, serve.

Nutritional information (per serving): 268 calories; 2.2 g fat; 57 g total carbs; 8.7 g protein

1. Mix chia seeds, coconut milk, quinoa, vanilla extract, cinnamon, and salt in a bowl. Cover with cling film and refrigerate overnight.

2. Add it to a pot and cook for 12 minutes.

3. Add walnuts and berries on top.

4. Once done, serve.

Nutritional information (per serving): 487 calories; 42 g fat; 25 g total carbs; 9 g protein

Overnight Coconut Quinoa

Cook Time: 20 minutes

Servings: 6

Ingredients:

- ¼ cup chia seeds
- 1/2 cup quinoa
- 1 cup unsweetened coconut milk
- Two teaspoons of vanilla extract
- ¼ teaspoon cinnamon
- ½ cup walnuts
- 1 ½ cups berries
- pinch of salt

Instructions:

Blueberry Banana Pancakes with Chunky Apple Compote

Cook Time: 10 minutes

Servings: 4

Ingredients:

- Three flax eggs
- Six bananas
- Two teaspoons of baking powder
- 1 ½ cups rolled oats
- Two ¼ cups of blueberries
- ¼ teaspoon salt
- Five dates pitted
- Two apples
- One tablespoon of lemon juice
- ¼ teaspoon cinnamon powder

Instructions:

1. Add

2. Fresh oats to your blender and then blend for 1 minute. Add flax eggs, bananas, baking powder, and salt to the blender. Pulse for 2 minutes.

3. Transfer it to a small glass bowl and add the blueberries. Let sit for 10 minutes.

4. Heat a saucepan and add a dollop of almond butter. Add a few spoons of the pancake mix and fry until golden at the bottom. Remove to a plate.

5. Core and chop apples. Add apples, dates, lemon juice, cinnamon powder, and a pinch of salt to a blender and two tablespoons of water. Blend well. Remove to a plate.

6. Serve pancakes with apple compote.

Nutritional information (per serving): 490 calories; 13 g fat; 35 g total carbs; 22 g protein

Toast with Beans and Avocado

Cook Time: 5 minutes

Servings: 2

Ingredients:

- 1 cup garbanzo beans
- Two spelled flour bread slices   *spelt*

- One avocado, sliced
- Salt, to taste
- white onion, sliced

Instructions:

1. Toast the bread slices. Add avocado and beans on top.

2. Add onions and sprinkle salt over it.

3. Serve and enjoy!

Nutritional information (per serving): 762 calories; 72 g fat; 13 g total carbs; 19 g protein

Morning Muesli

Cook Time: 35 minutes

Servings: 11

Ingredients:

- ½ cup amaranth oats
- 1 cup unsweetened coconut or almond milk
- One tablespoon of almonds, sliced
- ½ cup apple, chopped
- Dash of cinnamon

Instructions:

1. Mix all ingredients except almonds and apples in a bowl and refrigerate overnight.

2. Enjoy topped with almonds and apples!

Nutritional information (per serving): 218 calories; 12 g fat; 25 g total carbs; 5 g protein

Warm and Nutty Cinnamon Quinoa

Cook Time: 20 minutes

Servings: 4

Ingredients:

- 1 cup water
- 1 cup almond or coconut milk
- 2 cups blackberries
- 1 cup quinoa, organic
- 1/3 cup almonds, chopped and toasted
- 1/2 teaspoon cinnamon
- Four teaspoons of organic agave nectar

Instructions:

1. Mix water, quinoa, and milk in a pan. Bring to a boil over high heat. Reduce the heat, cover, and cook for 15 minutes.
2. Add cinnamon and blackberries and transfer to 4 bowls. Add almonds, and then add one teaspoon agave over each bowl. Serve and enjoy.

Nutritional information (per serving): 298 calories; 19 g fat; 16 g total carbs; 17 g protein

Quinoa Breakfast Patties

Cook Time: 25 minutes

Servings: 8

Ingredients:

- 2 cups vegetable broth
- 1 cup cooked quinoa

- Two flax eggs
- Two teaspoons parsley
- Two tablespoons of coconut oil
- Salt and pepper to taste

Instructions:

1. Rinse quinoa entirely and add to a pan with vegetable broth. Once it boils, reduce the heat and cook for 15 minutes.
2. Add quinoa, flax eggs, parsley, two tablespoons oil, salt, and pepper to a bowl and mix well to combine.
3. Add little olive oil to the pan. Shape the mixture into balls, place on the pan, and flatten with the palm of your hand. Cook for 3 minutes per side.
1. Top with parsley and serve. Enjoy!

Nutritional information (per serving): 225 calories; 6 g fat; 52 g total carbs; 9 g protein

Squash Breakfast Bowl

Cook Time: 1 hour 25 minutes

Servings: 2

Ingredients:

- 16 oz. squash
- Two tablespoons of almond butter
- Two tablespoons almonds, chopped
- Cinnamon, to taste

Instructions:

1. Preheat the oven to 400 F. Poke squash with a fork and wrap in foil. Bake for 15 minutes. Let cool, peel, and chop.
2. Mash the squash in a bowl, and add cinnamon. Add to a bowl and top with nuts. Add almond butter. Serve and enjoy!

Nutritional information (per serving): 445 calories; 35 g fat; 19 g total carbs; 14 g protein

Parsley Kale and Berry Smoothie

Cook Time: 5 minutes

Servings: 1

Ingredients:

- One banana, cut into pieces
- 1/2 cup flat-leaf parsley (leaves & stems), packed
- One teaspoon of ground flaxseed
- Four kale leaves, center ribs removed
- 1 cup water
- 1 cup organic berries, frozen

Instructions:

1. Add all the specific ingredients for the smoothie to a blender and puree until you add more water if too thick.
2. Pour into chilled glasses and serve immediately. Enjoy!

Nutritional information (per serving): 214 calories; 2.4 g fat; 49 g total carbs; 4 g protein

Quinoa Bowl with Avocado

Cook Time: 15 minutes

Servings: 4

Ingredients:

- One tablespoon of olive oil
- One teaspoon turmeric
- Four servings of quinoa, cooked
- One avocado
- Two tablespoons of almond butter
- salt and pepper, to taste

Instructions:

1. Cook quinoa according to package directions. Add butter and divide among four bowls.
2. Add 1/4 avocado and 1/4 tomato to each bowl. Season and serve.

Nutritional information (per serving): 311 calories; 16 g fat; 42 g total carbs; 13 g protein

Green Apple Smoothie

Cook Time: 5 minutes

Servings: 1

Ingredients:

- 4 Medrol dates
- One green apple
- 3 cups spinach
- ½ cup water
- One teaspoon of lemon juice
- Eight ice cubes

Instructions:

1. Core the apple and slice it into chunks. Remove pits from dates.
2. Add all ingredients to a blender and blend well.
3. Add lemon juice and blend again. Enjoy!

Nutritional information (per serving): 210 calories; 3 g fat; 7 g total carbs; 3 g protein

Creamed Turnips and Greens

Cook Time: 20 minutes

Servings: 6

Ingredients:

- One lb. turnips, peeled and cut into wedges
- 4 cups turnip greens, chopped
- Two tablespoons of extra-virgin olive oil
- ½ cup water
- Two tablespoons of spelled flour
- 1 ½ cups almond milk
- ½ teaspoon ground nutmeg
- ⅛ teaspoon ground white pepper
- Salt, to taste

Instructions:

1. Preheat oil in an s
2. mall-sized skillet over medium heat. Add turnips, water, and salt, cover, and bring to a boil.
3. Uncover the skillet, add greens and cook for 10 to 15 minutes. Add more water if the greens begin to stick.
4. Add flour, increase the heat and cook for 30

seconds. Add milk, nutmeg, white pepper, and more salt. Cook for 3-4 minutes, stirring often. Serve topped with lemon zest.

Nutritional information: 243 calories; 17 g fat; 5 g total carbs; 17 g protein

Breakfast Hash

Cook Time: 1 hour

Servings: 6

Ingredients:

- Three squash diced
- One teaspoon of dried thyme
- 1/4 cup + 1 teaspoon olive oil
- One onion, diced
- Salt and pepper to taste

Instructions:

1. Add squash, 1/4 cup olive oil, and spices to a bowl and mix well. Bake in a casserole dish at 450 F for 15 minutes. Stir every 5 minutes.
2. Add olive oil to a small-sized skillet and cook the onion for 8 minutes. Season to taste.
3. Add squash to the onion mixture and mix well to combine. Cook for 1-2 minutes.
4. Serve and enjoy.

Nutritional information (per serving): 202 calories; 13 g fat; 12 g total carbs; 10 g protein

Kale, Tahini, and Bell Pepper Wraps

Cook Time: 10 minutes

Servings: 2

Ingredients:

- Two spelled flour tortillas
- 1/2 cup tahini
- One red bell pepper, sliced
- 1 cup kale

Instructions:

1. Spread tahini on top of each tortilla.
2. Top with the remaining ingredients and roll into burritos. Secure with toothpicks and serve.

Nutritional information (per serving): 209 calories; 11 g fat; 15 g total carbs; 18 g protein

Breakfast Kamut

Cook Time: 5 minutes

Servings: 2

Ingredients:

- 1 cup (7 oz) Kamut berries, milled
- 3 3/4 cups unsweetened almond milk
- 1/2 teaspoon salt
- One tablespoon of almond butter
- Four tablespoons of agave syrup

Instructions:

1. Add the Kamut, almond milk, and salt in a medium saucepan, and stir to incorporate. First, bring to a boil, then reduce heat to medium and simmer for about 10 minutes.
2. Take off the heat and mix well in the butter and agave nectar.

Nutritional information (per serving): 194 calories; 11 g fat; 10 g total carbs; 14 g protein

Creamy Vanilla Matcha Amaranth

Cook Time: 20 minutes

Servings: 2

Ingredients:

- 1 ½ cup water
- ½ cup amaranth
- ¼ cup almond milk
- ½ teaspoon vanilla extract
- One teaspoon of matcha powder
- One tablespoon of agave syrup
- One tablespoon of hemp seeds
- pinch of salt

Instructions:

1. Add 1 ½ cups water to a pot and bring to a boil.
2. Add amaranth and a pinch of salt. Reduce heat, cover it, and cook for 15 minutes.
3. Turn the heat off and add almond milk, matcha powder, vanilla extract, and agave syrup. Mix well to combine.
4. Divide into two bowls and top with hemp seeds and fruits, and serve.

Nutritional information: 240 calories; 11 g fat; 31 g total carbs; 5 g protein

Blackberry Breakfast Bars

Cook Time: 20 minutes

Servings: 8

Ingredients:

- Four baby bananas
- 2 cups quinoa
- 1 cup spelled flour
- ½ cup grapeseed oil
- ¼ cup agave nectar
- ¼ teaspoon sea salt
- Organic blackberry jam

Instructions:

1. Preheat the oven to 350°F. Mash baby bananas in a bowl.
2. Add grapeseed oil and agave nectar to bananas and mix well.
3. Add quinoa, sea salt, and spelled flour. Mix well until dough is formed. Press it into a baking pan.
4. Add jam on top and crumble the remaining dough on top.
5. Bake for 20 minutes and serve!

Nutritional information (per serving): 471 calories; 16 g fat; 76 g total carbs; 6 g protein

Cardamom and Apple Quinoa Porridge

Cook Time: 20 minutes

Servings: 2

Ingredients:

- 1 cup quinoa
- Four cardamom pods
- Two apples, cut into slices
- One teaspoon of agave syrup
- 8 1/2 oz. almond milk

Instructions:

1. Add cardamom and quinoa to a pan with 9 oz. Water and 3 1/2 oz. Milk.
1. Add the remaining milk and cook for 5 minutes. Remove the cardamom pods, divide the mixture among bowls and add peaches and agave syrup. Serve and enjoy.

Nutritional information (per serving): 501 calories; 10 g fat; 23 g total carbs; 17 g protein

Arugula and Avocado Breakfast Sandwich

Cook Time: 20 minutes

Servings: 2

Ingredients:

- ¼ cup almond yogurt
- Four slices spelled flour bread, toasted
- 1 cup arugula
- One avocado, peeled, pitted, and sliced
- One tablespoon pepitas

- salt and pepper

Instructions:

1. Season yogurt with salt and pepper.
2. Place two bread slices on two plates. Add an even layer of yogurt sauce to the toast.
3. Add a portion of arugula and avocado on top, along with pepitas. Top with another bread slice. Slice sandwich.
4. Once done, serve.

Nutritional information (per serving): 131 calories; 5 g fat; 14 g total carbs; 8 g protein

Cinnamon and Almond Porridge

Cook Time: 10 minutes

Servings: 4

Ingredients:

- 2 cups almond milk
- 2 cups water
- Two teaspoons of agave syrup
- 2 cups amaranth
- ¼ teaspoon vanilla extract
- ½ cup almonds
- ½ teaspoon ground cinnamon
- ¼ teaspoon salt

Instructions:

1. Add all ingredients except almonds and cinnamon to a pan, heat over medium heat, and stir well. Bring the mixture to a simmer. Cook for 5 minutes, stirring often.

2. Add almonds and cinnamon on top.
3. Once done, serve.

Nutritional information (per serving): 239 calories; 11 g fat; 44 g total carbs; 10 g protein

Green Almond Smoothie

Preparation time: 5 minutes

Servings: 1

Ingredients

- One banana, frozen
- 1 cup coconut milk, unsweetened
- ¼ cup or one scoop of protein powder
- Two tablespoons of almond butter
- 2 cups kale
- 1 cup ice

Instructions

1. Add all the specific ingredients for the smoothie to a blender and blend until smooth.
2. Pour into chilled glasses and serve immediately. Enjoy!

Nutritional information (per serving): 238 calories; 15.8 g fat; 8 g total carbs; 14 g protein

Almond Flour Muffins

Cook Time: 30 minutes

Servings: 12

Ingredients:

- 1 cup blanched almond flour

- Two flax eggs
- One tablespoon of agave nectar
- ¼ teaspoon baking soda
- ½ teaspoon apple cider vinegar

Instructions:

1. Mix soda and flour in a bowl. Mix flax eggs, nectar, and vinegar in a separate bowl.
2. Combine both mixtures and stir well.
3. Preheat the oven to 350 F, and pour the mixture into muffin tins. Bake for 15 minutes. Enjoy!

Nutritional information (per serving): 555 calories; 2 g fat; 115 g total carbs; 16 g protein

Roasted Red Rose Potatoes and Kale Breakfast Hash

Cook Time: 45 minutes

Servings: 2

Ingredients:

- Two tablespoons of coconut oil, melted
- Two red rose potatoes
- One teaspoon of coconut sugar
- One red onion, skin, and tops removed and sliced into wedges lengthwise
- 1/8 teaspoon ground turmeric
- One bundle of kale, chopped and large stems removed
- ½ teaspoon each salt and pepper
- Two tablespoons of fresh parsley

Instructions:

1. Season red rose potatoes with ½ tablespoon oil, coconut sugar, and a pinch of salt and pepper. Toss to coat. Bake onions and potatoes for 35 minutes, flipping halfway. Remove from oven and set aside.
2. Add pressed tofu to a bowl and crumble it into small pieces. Season with turmeric, parsley, a pinch of salt, and pepper. Set aside.
3. Heat a skillet over medium-high heat. Add tofu, ½ tablespoon oil, and one teaspoon of tandoori masala spice. Cook for 5 minutes, stirring occasionally. Remove from skillet and set aside.
4. Add the olive oil to the small skillet and add kale to it. Season with one teaspoon of tandoori masala spice, salt, and pepper. Cook for 4 minutes, stirring frequently.
5. Turn the heat off but keep it over the burner.
6. Divide kale between 2 plates and top with onion and roasted red rose potatoes. Add remaining parsley on top. Serve.

Nutritional information (per serving): 355 calories; 15.7 g fat; 37.3 g total carbs; 15.7 g protein

Date and Almond Porridge

Cook Time: 10 minutes

Servings: 1

Ingredients:

- 1 Medjool date, chopped
- Six ¾ oz. almond milk
- One teaspoon of almond butter
- ½ cup buckwheat flakes

- ¼ cup strawberries, hulled

Instructions:

1. Add the date and milk to a pan. Heat gently and add the buckwheat flakes and cook for a few minutes.
2. Add in butter and top with strawberries. Serve.

Nutritional information (per serving): 306 calories; 10.7 g fat; 47 g total carbs; 10 g protein

Almond Biscuits

Cook Time: 25 minutes

Servings: 8

Ingredients:

- 1 cup almond milk
- 2 cups almond flour
- One tablespoon of baking powder
- ½ teaspoon baking soda
- One tablespoon of lemon juice
- A pinch of salt
- Four tablespoons of almond butter

Instructions:

1. Preheat your oven to 455 F and grease a baking sheet with oil.
1. Mix all dry ingredients in a bowl. Add butter and mix well to make crumbles.
2. Add all wet ingredients and stir well to combine. Knead for 7-10 minutes.
3. Shape into biscuits and bake on the baking sheet for 10-15 minutes.

Nutritional information (per serving): 360 calories; 27.3 g fat; 10 g total carbs; 19 g protein

Red rose potato Toasts

Cook Time: 15 minutes

Servings: 8-10

Ingredients:

- One tablespoon of avocado oil
- Two red rose potatoes, sliced
- One teaspoon salt

Instructions:

1. Get a baking sheet ready and turn the oven on to 425 degrees Fahrenheit.
2. Spread the potato slices on the parchment paper, leaving some room between them, and grease both sides with the avocado oil.
3. Season with salt. Put it in the oven for 5 to 6 minutes, flip it over, and bake for another 5 minutes. Enjoy!

Nutritional information (per serving): 215 calories;6 g fat; 10 g total carbs; 9 g protein

Vegetable Rose Potato

Cook time: 20 minutes

Servings: 4

Ingredients

- Four red rose potatoes
- Six leaves of Lacinato kale, stemmed, chopped

- Two tablespoons of olive oil
- One onion, chopped
- One green bell pepper, diced
- One teaspoon of smoked paprika
- One teaspoon of seasoning, salt-free
- Ground pepper, and salt, to taste

Instructions

1. Microwave the fresh potatoes until done but still firm. Finely chop them when cool.
2. Preheat oil in a skillet over medium heat. Sauté onions until translucent. Add potatoes and bell pepper, and sauté, stirring over medium-high heat until golden brown.
3. Stir in the kale and seasoning, then cook, constantly stirring, until the mixture is a bit browned. Occasionally add water to prevent sticking if necessary.
4. Sprinkle with pepper and salt to taste. Serve hot.

Nutritional information (per serving): 337 calories; 7.4 g fat; 63 g total carbs; 8 g protein

Kale Brussels Sprouts Salad

Cook Time: 20 minutes

Servings: 2

Ingredients:

- One bunch of curly green kale stems removed, chopped
- ¼ cup almonds, sliced
- ½ lb. Brussels sprouts, shredded

- Two teaspoons of white miso
- ¼ cup tahini
- Two tablespoons of white wine vinegar
- Two teaspoons of agave syrup
- ¼ cup water
- A pinch of red pepper flakes
- Salt, to taste

Instructions:

1. Season kale with salt and drizzle with salt. Massage until kale becomes darker in color. Transfer kale to a bowl.
2. Whisk vinegar, tahini, agave syrup, miso, and red pepper flakes in a bowl.
3. Whisk in the water until creamy, and add this dressing over sprouts and kale.
4. Toast almonds in a pan over medium heat until fragrant.
5. Add toasted almonds to the salad and toss. Once done, serve and enjoy.

Nutritional information (per serving): 411 calories; 26.5 g fat; 33 g total carbs; 18 g protein

Rice Arugula Salad

Cook time: 7 minutes

Servings: 2

Ingredients

- 1 cup wild rice, cooked
- One handful of arugula washed
- ¾ cup almonds

- Six sun-dried tomatoes in oil, chopped
- Three tablespoons of olive oil
- One onion
- Pepper and salt, to taste

Instructions

1. Place a saucepan over low heat and roast the almonds for 3 minutes. Transfer to a salad bowl.
2. Sauté onions in 1/3 olive oil for 3 minutes on low heat. Add dried tomatoes and cook for about 2 minutes. Transfer to a bowl.
3. Add the remaining olive oil to the pan and fry the bread until crunchy. Sprinkle with pepper and salt. Set aside.
4. Add arugula to the bowl containing sautéed tomato mixture. Add wild rice and toss to combine. Season with pepper and salt.

Nutritional information (per serving): 688 calories; 37.7 g fat; 56 g total carbs; 19 g protein

Tomato Salad

Cook time: 15 minutes

Servings: 4

Ingredients

- One head of romaine lettuce, washed, chopped
- One avocado, sliced
- 24 cherry tomatoes
- ½ cup cilantro, chopped
- Fresh lime juice for dressing

Instructions

1. Divide all the ingredients between 4 plates and drizzle with lime juice dressing.
2. Toss well to combine. Enjoy immediately.

Nutritional information (per serving): 203 calories; 16.2 g fat; 12 g total carbs; 6 g protein

Kale Apple Roasted Root Vegetable Salad

Cook Time: 30 minutes

Servings: 6

Ingredients

- 1 ½ cups parsnips, turnips, and red rose potatoes, diced
- 8 cups kale, chopped
- ½ cup apple chunks
- Two tablespoons of apple cider vinegar
- ½ teaspoon cinnamon
- ½ teaspoon turmeric
- Four tablespoons of olive oil divided
- Salt and pepper to taste

Instructions

1. Place a skillet over medium heat. Add vinegar, apple, cinnamon, turmeric, and salt. Bring the mixture to a boil and set aside.
2. Preheat the oven to 350 F. Preheat oil in a cast iron pan over medium heat.
3. Add parsnips, turnips and red rose potatoes, and cook for about 5 minutes.

4. Transfer to the preheated oven and roast for about 10 minutes.

5. Place a skillet over medium heat. Add the remaining olive oil

6. To the skillet, add the kale and apples and cook for about 4 minutes

7. Add the parsnips, turnips, red rose potatoes, and vinegar mixture to the skillet. Cook for about 5 minutes. Add salt and pepper to taste.

8. Serve while hot, and enjoy!

Nutritional Info (per serving): 128 calories; 16 g fat; 32 g total carbs; 3 g protein

Rice Arugula Salad with Sesame Garlic Dressing

Cook Time: 1 hour

Servings: 4

Ingredients

- 1 cup wild rice, cooked
- 1/8 teaspoon cumin
- ½ bunch of arugula, chopped
- Two tablespoons parsley, chopped
- Two tablespoons basil, chopped
- Salt and black pepper to taste

For the dressing:

- One head of garlic, roasted and peeled
- ½ cup apple juice
- ¼ cup lemon juice
- ¼ cup tahini
- ¼ cup virgin olive oil
- Salt, to taste

Instructions

1. Combine all the dressing's components in a blender and process until completely smooth and creamy. Putting aside.

2. Place a stockpot over medium-high heat. Season rice with cumin and salt. Set aside to chill for about 10 minutes.

3. Add arugula, parsley, basil, olives, salt, and pepper to the bowl. Serve and enjoy!

Nutritional Info (per serving): 447 calories; 44.4 g fat; 43 g total carbs; 19 g protein

Roasted Lemon Asparagus Watercress Salad

Cook Time: 10 minutes

Servings: 4

Ingredients

- 2 cups asparagus, ends trimmed
- 2 cups watercress
- 2 cups baby spinach
- One lemon, sliced, seeded
- One onion, sliced
- 1/8 teaspoon cayenne
- Two tablespoons of olive oil
- Salt and pepper to taste

Instructions

1. Preheat olive oil. Add the clean asparagus and cook for about 5 minutes. Set aside.
2. Return the skillet to medium-low heat. Add the remaining olive oil.
3. Add onion and lemon slices and cook for about 5 minutes. Remove from heat and season with salt, cayenne, and pepper.
4. Add the spinach to a large bowl. Add cooked onion and lemon slices on top. Finally, add the asparagus.
5. Serve and enjoy!

Nutritional Info (per serving): 129 calories; 7 g fat; 11 g total carbs; 5 g protein

Pumpkin and Brussels Sprouts Mix

Cook time: 35 minutes

Servings: 8

Ingredients:

- 1 lb. Brussels sprouts halved
- One pumpkin, peeled, cubed
- Four garlic cloves, sliced
- Two tablespoons of fresh parsley, chopped
- Two tablespoons of balsamic vinegar
- 1/3 cup olive oil
- Salt

1.
2. pepper
3. Instructions:
4. Preheat your oven. Be sure to spray your baking dish entirely with cooking spray before beginning.
5. Combine pumpkin seeds, garlic, and sprouts in a bowl. Pour oil over the vegetables and toss to coat.
6. Transfer to the baking dish and cook for 35-40 minutes. Stir once halfway.
7. Serve topped with parsley.

Nutritional Info (per serving): 152 calories; 9 g fat; 17 g carbohydrate; 4 g protein

Almond and Tomato Salad

Cook Time: 12 minutes

Servings: 4

Ingredients:

- 1 cup arugula/ rocket
- 7 oz fresh tomatoes, sliced or chopped
- Two teaspoons of olive oil
- 2 cups kale
- 1/2 cup almonds

Instructions:

1. Add and heat olive oil.
2. Add tomatoes to the pan and fry for about 10 minutes. Once cooked, allow it to cool.
3. Combine all fresh ingredients in a glass bowl and serve.

Nutritional Info (per serving): 355 calories; 19.1 g fat; 8.3 g carbohydrate; 33 g protein; 135 mg sodium; 2 g fiber

Strawberry Spinach Salad

Cook time: 10 minutes

Servings: 4

Ingredients:

- 5 cups of baby spinach
- 2 cups strawberries, sliced
- Two tablespoons of lemon juice
- 1/2 teaspoon Dijon mustard
- 1/4 cup olive oil
- 3/4 cup toasted almonds, chopped
- 1/4 red onion, sliced
- Salt, and pepper, to taste

Instructions:

1. Take a large bowl, mix Dijon mustard with lemon juice, and slowly add olive oil and combine. Season the mixture with black pepper and salt.
2. Mix strawberries, half a cup of almonds, and sliced onion in a bowl.
3. Pour the fresh dressing on top and toss to combine. Serve the salad topped with almonds and vegan cheese.

Nutritional information: 116 calories; 3 g fat; 13 g total carbs; 6 g protein

Apple Spinach Salad

Cook time: 10 minutes

Servings: 4

Ingredients:

- 5 ounces of fresh spinach
- 1/4 red onion, sliced
- One apple, sliced
- 1/4 cup sliced toasted almonds
  For the Dressing:
- Three tablespoons of red wine vinegar
- 1/3 cup olive oil
- One minced garlic clove
- Two teaspoons of Dijon mustard
- Salt, and pepper, to taste

Instructions:

1. Combine wine vinegar, olive oil, garlic, and Dijon mustard in a bowl. Season with black pepper and salt.
2. Mix fresh spinach, apple, onion, and toasted almonds in a separate bowl. Pour the new dressing on top and toss to combine. Serve

Nutritional information (per serving): 232 calories; 20.8 g fat; 10 g total carbs; 3 g protein

Kale Power Salad

Cook Time: 40 minutes

Servings: 2

Ingredients:

- One bunch of kale, ribs removed and chopped
- 1/2 cup quinoa
- One tablespoon of olive oil
- 1/2 lime, juiced
- ½ teaspoon salt
- One tablespoon of olive oil
- One red rose potato, cut into small cubes
- One teaspoon of ground cumin
- 3/4 teaspoons salt
- 1/2 teaspoon smoked paprika
- One lime, juiced
- One avocado, sliced into long strips
- One tablespoon of olive oil
- One tablespoon of cilantro leaves
- One jalapeno, deseeded, membranes removed and chopped
- salt
- ¼ cup pepitas

Instructions:

1. You should give quinoa a 2-minute rinse in a colander under running water.
2. Rinsed quinoa should be added to two cups of water in a pot and cooked at a low simmer for 15 minutes. Take quinoa from the heat and cover it so it can rest for 5 minutes. Remove the

lid, let the excess water evaporate, and fluff the quinoa with a fork. Leave to cool.

3. Olive oil should be warmed in a pan over medium heat. The red rose potatoes should be added and tossed in at this point.

4. Add smoked paprika, cumin, and salt. Mix to combine.

5. Add ¼ cup of water once the pan is sizzling. Cover the pan and reduce heat to low. Cook for 10 minutes, stirring occasionally. Uncover the pan, raise the heat to medium, and cook for 7 minutes. Set aside to cool.

6. Transfer kale to a bowl, add salt and massage with your hands. Scrunch handfuls of kale in your hands, and repeat until kale is darker in color.

7. Mix 2 tablespoons olive oil, ½ teaspoon salt, and one lime juice in a bowl. Add over the kale and toss to coat.

8. Add two avocados, two lime juices, two tablespoons of olive oil, jalapeno, cilantro leaves, and salt in a blender. Blend well and season the avocado sauce.

9. Toast pepitas in a skillet over medium-low heat for 5 minutes, stirring frequently.

10. Add quinoa to the kale bowl and toss to combine well. Divide the kale and quinoa mixture into four bowls.

11. Top with red rose potatoes, avocado sauce, and pepitas. Enjoy!

Nutritional information: 250 calories; 11 g fat; 25 g total carbs; 9 g protein

Falafel Kale Salad with Tahini Dressing

Cook time: 5 minutes
Servings: 4
Ingredients

- 12 balls Vegan Falafels
- 6 cups kale, chopped
- 1/2 red onion, thinly sliced
- Two slices of pita bread, cut into squares
- One jalapeño, chopped
- Tahini Dressing
- 1-2 lemons, juiced

Instructions

1. In a mixing bowl, combine kale and lemon juice and toss well to mix. Place into the refrigerator.

2. Divide kale among four bowls. Top with three Falafel balls, red onion, jalapeño, and pita slices.

3. Top with tahini dressing and serve.

Nutritional information (per serving): 178 calories; 2.8 g fat; 16 g total carbs; 4 g protein

Fig and Kale Salad

Cook Time: 15 minutes

Servings: 2

Ingredients:

- One ripe avocado
- Two tablespoons of lemon juice
- 3 ½ oz kale, packed, stems removed, and cut into large-sized bits
- One carrot, shredded

- One yellow zucchini, diced
- Four fresh figs
- ¼ cup ground flaxseed
- 1 cup mixed green leaves
- One teaspoon of sea salt

Instructions:

1. Add kale to a bowl with avocado, lemon juice, and sea salt. Massage together until kale wilts.
2. Add in zucchini, carrot, and 2 cups of mixed green leaves.
3. Fold in figs and remaining ingredients. Toss and serve.

Nutritional information (per serving): 255 calories; 12.5 g fat; 35 g total carbs; 6 g protein

Cucumber Avocado Toast

Cook Time: 5 minutes

Servings: 2

Ingredients

- One cucumber, sliced
- Two sprouted (Essene) bread slices, toasted
- ¼ handful of basil leaves, chopped
- Four tablespoons avocado, mashed
- Salt and pepper to taste
- One teaspoon of lemon juice

Instructions

1. Combine lemon juice with the mashed avocado, then spread the mixture on two bread slices.
2. Top with cucumber slices along with the finely chopped basil leaves. Generously sprinkle with salt and pepper, and enjoy!

Nutritional information (per serving): 232 calories; 14 g fat; 24 g total carbs; 5 g protein

Kale and Cucumber Salad

Cook Time: 60 minutes

Servings: 2

Ingredients:

- One garlic clove
- 3 ½ oz fresh ginger
- 1/2 green Thai chili
- 1 ½ tablespoons sugar
- 1 ½ tablespoons fish sauce
- 1 ½ tablespoon vegetable oil
- 1 English cucumber, thinly sliced
- One bunch of red Russian kale, ribs, and stems removed, leaves torn into small pieces
- 1 Persian cucumber, thinly sliced
- Two tablespoons of fresh lime juice
- One small red onion, sliced
- One teaspoon sugar
- Two tablespoons of cilantro, chopped
- Salt, to taste

Instructions:

1. Heat the broiler and broil ginger with skin for 50 minutes, turning once. Let cool and slice.

2. Blend chile, ginger, garlic, sugar, fish sauce, oil, and two tablespoons of water in a blender until the paste forms.

3. Toss ¼ cup dressing and kale in a bowl and coat well. Massage with hands until kale softens.

4. Toss Persian and English cucumbers, lime juice, onion, and sugar in a bowl and season with salt. Let it sit for 10 minutes.

5. Add the cucumber mixture to the bowl with the kale and toss to combine.

6. Top with cilantro and serve.

Nutritional information (per serving): 160 calories; 8 g fat; 22 g total carbs; 3 g protein

Mexican Quinoa

Cook Time: 25 minutes

Servings: 4

Ingredients

- 1 cup quinoa, uncooked and rinsed
- 1 ½ cup vegetable broth
- 3 cups diced tomatoes
- 2 cups frozen corn
- 1 cup fresh parsley, chopped
- One onion, chopped
- Three cloves of garlic, minced
- Two bell peppers, chopped
- One tablespoon of paprika powder
- ½ tablespoon cumin
- Two tablespoons of olive oil
- Two tablespoons of lime juice

- Two green onions, chopped
- salt and pepper

Instructions

1. Place a large pot over medium heat. Add olive oil. Cook onions for 3 minutes.

2. Add garlic and peppers and cook for 5 minutes.

3. Add the remaining ingredients, including lime juice, green onions, and parsley. Cover and cook for about 20 minutes. Keep checking to make sure the quinoa doesn't stick and burn.

4. Add lime juice, green onions, and parsley.

Nutritional information (per serving): 231 calories; 17.8 g fat; 19 g total carbs; 2 g protein

Mediterranean Parsley Salad

Cook Time: 15 minutes

Servings: 2

Ingredients:

- ½ red onion, thinly sliced
- 1 cups parsley, chopped
- 1 Roma tomato, seeded and diced
- Six mints, chopped
- Three tablespoons of currants died
- One green chili, minced
- One tablespoon lemon
- Two tablespoons of olive oil
- 1/8 teaspoon sumac

- 1/8 teaspoon pepper, cracked
- ¼ teaspoon salt

Instructions:

1. Mix lemon juice, olive oil, sumac, salt, and pepper in a bowl and whisk to combine well.
2. Toss parsley with the remaining ingredients in a separate bowl.
3. Add the olive oil mixture to it and toss well and serve.

Nutritional information (per serving): 110 calories; 8 g fat; 7 g total carbs; 1 g protein

Tomatoes Parsley Salad

Cook Time: 10 minutes

Servings: 2

Ingredients:

- 2 cups curly parsley leaves, packed
- One teaspoon of garlic, minced
- 3/4 cup oil-packed sundried tomatoes, drained and julienned
- Two tablespoons of olive oil
- ½ cup basil leaves
- Two tablespoons of rice vinegar
- One shallot, minced
- One garlic clove, minced
- Salt and black pepper to taste

Instructions:

1. Wash parsley, dry, and add to a bowl. Add garlic and tomatoes. Toss well.

2. Wash the basil and dry it. Add it to a blender and add vinegar, oil, salt, and pepper. Blend until smooth.
3. Add garlic and shallots to the dressing.
4. Add the dressing over the salad and toss well. Divide among six salad plates and serve.

Nutritional information (per serving): 245 calories; 19.8 g fat; 12 g total carbs; 7 g protein

Lemon Parsley Quinoa Salad

Cook Time: 30 minutes

Servings: 2

Ingredients:

- One tablespoon of lemon juice
- 3 cups quinoa, cooked
- ¼ cup olive oil
- 1 ½ teaspoon lemon zest
- 1 cup Italian flat-leaf parsley, tightly packed
- ½ bell pepper, diced
- Salt and black pepper to taste

Instructions:

1. Cook quinoa according to package instructions. Add some water and heat in a microwave.
2. Mix lemon juice and zest in a bowl and whisk in olive oil.
3. Add salt and pepper.
4. Add parsley, rice, and diced pepper. Mix well and Enjoy!

Nutritional information (per serving): 207 calories; 9 g fat; 28 g total carbs; 2.6 g protein

Quinoa and Parsley Salad

Cook Time: 25 minutes

Servings: 2

Ingredients:

- ½ cup quinoa, uncooked
- 1 cup water
- ¾ cup parsley leaves
- ½ cup celery, sliced
- ½ cup green onions, sliced
- Three tablespoons of fresh lemon juice
- ½ cup dried apricots, chopped
- One tablespoon of agave syrup
- One tablespoon of olive oil
- ¼ cup unsalted pumpkinseed kernels, toasted
- ¼ teaspoon salt
- ¼ teaspoon black pepper

Instructions:

1. Add fresh quinoa and water to a pan and bring to a boil. Cover, reduce heat, and simmer for 20 minutes. Add to a bowl and fluff with a fork.
2. Add celery, parsley, onions, and apricots.
3. Whisk olive oil, lemon juice, syrup, salt, and black pepper. Add to quinoa mixture and toss well.
4. Top with seeds and serve.

Nutritional information (per serving): 238 calories; 8.6 g fat; 35 g total carbs; 6 g protein

Summer Parsley Salad

Cook Time: 5 minutes

Servings: 2

Ingredients:

- One bunch of parsley, minced
- One tomato, cut into chunks
- Four baby cucumbers, sliced
- One red bell pepper, chopped
- Two tablespoons of olive oil
- One tablespoon of lemon juice
- One tablespoon of white vinegar
- One tablespoon of agave syrup
- One teaspoon salt

Instructions:

1. Add peppers, cucumbers, tomato, olives, and parsley to a bowl. Toss to combine.
2. Whisk vinegar, olive oil, lemon juice, agave syrup, and salt in a separate bowl and add over the salad. Toss well and serve. Enjoy!

Nutritional information (per serving): 280 calories; 18.6 g fat; 21 g total carbs; 9 g protein

Arugula-Zucchini Soup

Cook Time: 30 minutes

Servings: 4

Ingredients:

- One tablespoon of almond butter
- One tablespoon of olive oil

- Two garlic cloves minced
- Two leeks, white and green parts and halved lengthwise, rinsed
- 4 cups zucchini, chopped
- 6 cups vegetable broth
- 10 cups of baby arugula
- Two tablespoons of lemon juice
- 1/2 cup parsley, chopped
- 3/4 teaspoon salt
- 1/4 teaspoon ground pepper

Instructions:

1. Heat butter and some oil in a pot over medium heat. Add garlic and leeks and cook for 3 minutes. Add zucchini, broth, salt, and pepper, and bring to a boil. Reduce the heat, cover, and cook for 15 minutes. Remove from heat.
2. Add arugula and let stand for 5 minutes. Puree the soup with a blender. Add lemon juice and parsley. Serve and enjoy!

Nutritional information (per serving): 647 calories; 31.6 g fat; 7 g total carbs; 36 g protein

Potato and Parsley Soup

Cook Time: 40 minutes

Servings: 2

Ingredients:

- One onion, sliced
- One tablespoon oil
- One celery stick, diced

- One lb. potatoes, peeled and diced
- 4 cups vegetable stock
- Two tablespoons parsley
- Salt and pepper to taste

Instructions:

1. Onions should be added to olive oil that has been heated in a pan. Stirring often, cook over low heat for 10 minutes.
2. The dish would benefit from the addition of celery, potatoes, and half a bunch of parsley.
3. Turn the heat down low, add the stock, and bring it to a boil. Prepare in 15 minutes.
4. Add the remaining parsley and blend the mixture. Add more stock if required.
5. Season with salt and pepper and reheat. Enjoy!

Nutritional information (per serving): 240 calories; 7.2 g fat; 41 g total carbs; 5 g protein

Carrot and Parsley Soup

Cook Time: 22 minutes

Servings: 2

Ingredients:

- One bunch of flat-leaf parsley
- 1 oz almond butter
- Two celery stalks, chopped
- One tablespoon of olive oil
- One onion, diced
- One lb. carrots, roughly chopped
- 1 cup almond milk

- Three garlic cloves
- Three ¾ cups of vegetable stock

Instructions:

1. Melt some oil and butter in a pan and cook garlic, celery, and onions on low heat for 8 minutes.
2. Increase the heat, add carrots and cook for 2 minutes, stirring constantly.
3. Add chicken stock, bring to a boil, and cook for 10 minutes.
4. Add parsley and cook for 1 minute.
5. Let cool and add the mixture to a blender and blend until smooth.
6. Put on heat and add milk, and stir. Enjoy!

Nutritional information: 140 calories; 8 g fat; 12 g total carbs; 5 g protein

Fig and Arugula Salad

Cook Time: 15 minutes

Servings: 2

Ingredients:

- Three tablespoons of olive oil
- ½ cup walnut halves
- Two teaspoons of balsamic vinegar
- One teaspoon honey
- 5 oz fresh arugula
- ½ cup dried figs, quartered
- One carrot shaved

- 15 oz can unsalted chickpeas, drained and rinsed
- 3 oz goat cheese, crumbled
- 1/8 teaspoon cayenne pepper
- ¾ teaspoon + 1/8 teaspoon salt

Instructions:

1. Preheat the oven to 375 F.
2. Mix cayenne, walnuts, one tablespoon olive oil, and 1/8 teaspoon salt and spread on a baking sheet.
3. Whisk honey, balsamic vinegar, the remaining olive oil, and the remaining salt in a bowl.
4. Toss arugula, chickpeas, carrot, and figs in a separate bowl.
5. Top with toasted walnuts and goat cheese.
6. Add 2 cups of salad to each of the four bowls. Add dressing on top and serve.

Nutritional information (per serving): 403 calories; 24 g fat; 35 g total carbs; 13 g protein

Wild rice and Arugula Salad

Cook Time: 10 minutes

Servings: 2

Ingredients:

- ½ teaspoon Dijon mustard
- One tablespoon of olive oil
- ½ teaspoon lemon rind, grated
- One tablespoon of fresh lemon juice
- 1 cup wild rice, cooked

- 1 1/2 cups baby arugula, firmly packed
- 1/8 cup red onion, thinly sliced
- 3/8 teaspoon salt
- ¼ teaspoon black pepper

Instructions:

1. Mix lemon juice, rind, oil, mustard, salt, and pepper in a bowl and whisk well.
2. Add onions and wild rice and toss well.
3. Add arugula. Toss and serve.

Nutritional information (per serving): 152 calories; 7.7 g fat; 16 g total carbs; 5 g protein

Kale Soup

Cook Time: 1 hour

Servings: 2

Ingredients:

- One yellow onion, chopped
- Two tablespoons of olive oil
- Two tablespoons garlic, chopped
- 8 cups vegetable stock
- One bunch of kale stems was removed, and the leaves chopped
- Six white potatoes, peeled and cubed
- 15 oz can tomato, diced
- Two tablespoons of dried parsley
- One tablespoon of Italian seasoning
- Salt and pepper to taste

Instructions:

1. Heat olive oil in a soup pot. Cook garlic and onion in it until soft.
2. Add kale and cook for 2 minutes.
3. Add in vegetable stock, tomatoes, potatoes, parsley, and Italian seasoning. Cook soup over medium heat for 25 minutes. Season with salt and pepper. Serve and enjoy!

Nutritional information (per serving): 277 calories; 4.5 g fat; 51 g total carbs; 9.6 g protein

Lemon-Thyme Carrot Soup

Cook Time: 25 minutes

Servings: 8

Ingredients:

- 4 cups carrot slices
- Three tablespoons of lemon juice
- 5 cups vegetable stock
- 1 cup leeks, sliced
- Three teaspoons of dried thyme, crushed
- One bay leaf
- 1/8 teaspoon salt
- 1/8 teaspoon black pepper

Instructions:

1. Mix bay leaf, carrots, and leeks and stock in a pan. Bring to a boil over medium heat.
2. Add thyme, lemon juice, salt, and pepper. Cover and cook for 5 minutes.

3. Remove the bay leaf. Blend carrot mixture in a blender until smooth. Return pureed mixture to the pan and heat. Serve and enjoy!

Nutritional information (per serving): 246 calories; 10.4 g fat; 3 g total carbs; 33 g protein

Celery Parsley Soup

Cook Time: 30 minutes

Servings: 2

Ingredients:

- One tablespoon of olive oil
- Two tablespoons of almond butter
- Two leeks, white and light green portions only, sliced into half moons
- One bunch of celery, chopped
- One garlic clove, sliced
- One potato, peeled and diced
- Four handfuls of baby spinach
- ½ bunch of flat-leaf parsley leaves only
- Two tablespoons of lemon juice
- ½ cup vegan yogurt
- One teaspoon of coarse sea salt

Instructions:

1. Add butter to a pot and melt.
2. Add leeks, celery, and potato and cook for 6 minutes, stirring occasionally.
3. Add salt and garlic and cook for two more minutes.

4. Add 4 cups of warm water and bring to a boil. Reduce heat and cook for 10 minutes.
5. Add parsley and spinach to a blender and add the hot soup over it. Let cool and puree until smooth.
6. Add lemon juice and yogurt and blend again.
7. Add celery leaves over soup and serve.

Nutritional information (per serving): 150 calories; 7 g fat; 19 g total carbs; 4 g protein

Kale and Buckwheat Soup

Cook Time: 30 minutes

Servings: 2

Ingredients:

- 1 cup onion, chopped
- One tablespoon of vegetable oil
- One teaspoon of garlic, minced
- ¾ cup celery, chopped
- 4 cups vegetable stock
- 1/3 cup buckwheat groats
- 2 cups red rose potato, diced
- One bay leaf
- 2 cups kale, thinly sliced and ribs removed
- One tablespoon of fresh thyme
- Salt and pepper to taste

Instructions:

1. Heat a pan over medium-low heat. Add onion, oil, celery, and garlic. Cover and cook for 7 minutes.

2. Add water, stock, potato, bay leaf, kale, buckwheat, and thyme. Bring to a simmer and cover and cook for 17 minutes.

3. Add salt and pepper and serve.

Nutritional information: 239 calories; 7 g fat; 30 g total carbs; 15.5 g protein

Wild rice and Buckwheat Soup

Cook Time: 2 hours

Servings: 2

Ingredients:

- One onion, grated
- 1 cup brown wild rice
- One tablespoon of olive oil
- Two bay leaves
- One carrot, grated
- ¾ cup raw buckwheat groats
- 4 ½ cup vegetable broth
- Three tablespoons of olive oil
- 9 oz pack of fresh baby spinach

Instructions:

1. Soak wild rice in cold water for 1 hour. Drain and set aside.

2. Heat oil in a stew pot over medium heat.

3. Add bay leaves and wild rice and stir well.

4. Add in 3 cups vegetable broth, stir and bring to a boil. Cook on slow boil for 10 minutes.

5. Reduce heat to simmer and add buckwheat. Cook for 25 minutes.

6. Add the remaining broth. Remove from heat.

7. Add in spinach. Discard bay leaves. Divide among six bowls.

8. Add ½ tablespoon oil over each bowl and serve.

Nutritional information (per serving): 224 calories; 10 g fat; 29 g total carbs; 7.2 g protein

Butternut Squash and Turmeric Soup

Cook time: 25 minutes

Servings: 4

Ingredients:

- 2 1/2 lbs. butternut squash, cut into one-inch pieces
- 2 ½ tablespoons olive oil
- One onion, chopped
- One tablespoon vegetable bouillon base
- Two carrots, chopped
- Two tablespoons of coconut milk
- Two ¼ teaspoons of turmeric
- Two ¼ teaspoons of black pepper

Instructions:

1. Bring six cups of warm water to a boil, mix in vegetable bouillon base, and stir to make a broth.

2. Preheat a Dutch oven, add oil and onion and cook for 6-8 minutes. Add butternut squash and carrots with two teaspoons of turmeric and half a teaspoon of black pepper, and cook for one minute.

3. Add the broth and reduce the heat to low; cook for 20-22 minutes until the vegetables are tender.

4. Puree the soup, add coconut milk and serve.

Nutritional information (per serving): 226 calories; 9.2 g fat; 38 g total carbs; 3 g protein

Kale Crisps with Paprika Salt

Cook Time: 30 minutes

Servings: 6

Ingredients:

- ½ lb. kale leaves washed thoroughly
- ¼ teaspoon hot smoked paprika
- ½ teaspoon cumin
- One teaspoon of sea salt flakes
- Olive oil

Instructions:

1. Preheat the oven to 375 F. Cut stalks from the center of the kale leaves and discard. Chop the leaves into pieces. Completely dry the kale leaves and add to a bowl. Add one tablespoon of olive oil on top and toss to coat well.

2. Bake for 30 minutes. Mix salt, cumin, and paprika in a bowl and add over the kale. Serve.

Nutritional information (per serving): 37 calories; 2.2 g fat; 2.9 g total carbs; 1.5 g protein

Nutritional Yeast Pasta

Cook Time: 15 minutes

Servings: 2

Ingredients

- 8 oz pasta, cooked
- One tablespoon of olive oil
- One teaspoon of all-purpose flour
- 2/3 cup soy milk
- ¼ cup nutritional yeast
- ½ teaspoon mustard
- ½ teaspoon garlic powder
- Salt, to taste

Instructions

1. Place the cooked pasta in a bowl. Preheat oil in a saucepan over medium-low heat. Add flour and stir well to make a paste.

2. Slowly add the soy milk and stir well to combine. Add the nutritional yeast, mustard, garlic, and salt. Mix well to combine.

3. Add the cooked pasta. Stir for about 2 minutes. Enjoy!

Nutrition Info (per serving): 473 calories; 8 g fat; 85 g total carbs; 14 g protein

Agave Glazed Tofu

Cook time: 12 minutes

Servings: 2

Ingredients

- One block (12 oz.) of firm tofu, drained
- Three tablespoons of agave syrup
- ¼ cup soy sauce

- Three tablespoons of rice vinegar
- ½ cup canola oil
- One ½-inch ginger, thinly sliced
- ½ teaspoon crushed red pepper flakes

Instructions

1. Drain the excess moisture from the tofu. Slice tofu into nine pieces.

2. Mix agave syrup, soy sauce, rice vinegar, ginger, and red pepper flakes in a small bowl.

3. Add olive oil and heat it. Once heated up, add tofu and cook without stirring for 4 minutes on each side. Remove tofu.

4. Pour the maple mixture into the skillet, reduce the heat to medium and cook for 4 minutes. Serve and enjoy.

Red rose potato Squash

Cook time: 60 minutes

Servings: 4

Ingredients

- One lb. red rose potatoes, peeled, cut
- One butternut squash, peeled, deseeded, sliced
- 14 oz tin tomatoes, chopped
- 10 ½ oz. black rice to serve
- Two tablespoons of vegetable oil
- 14 oz tin coconut milk
- 12 oz. vegetable stock
- One red onion, quartered
- Three red chilies stalks were removed, cut into three
- Two garlic cloves halved
- 2 oz fresh ginger, peeled, thickly sliced
- One teaspoon of ground turmeric

- ½ teaspoon ground cinnamon
- One teaspoon of ground coriander
- One teaspoon of sea salt

Instructions

1. In a food processor, pulse onions, chilies, garlic, ginger, ground coriander, turmeric, cinnamon, and salt until processed.

2. Heat olive oil in a casserole dish. Add the onion mixture and sauté, stirring correctly, for 1 minute.

3. Stir in the vegetable stock, coconut milk, tinned tomatoes, squash, and potato, then bring to a boil. If more flavoring is desired, feel free to add it. Take away from the heat and wait 10 minutes. Enjoy!

Simple Quinoa Fried Rice

Cook Time: 20 minutes

Servings: 2

Ingredients

- 2 cups quinoa, cooked
- One tablespoon of olive oil
- Two carrots, chopped
- One small head of broccoli, chopped into florets
- One garlic clove, minced
- One teaspoon of red pepper flakes
- 1 ½ tablespoons soy sauce
- Two teaspoons of rice wine vinegar
- Two teaspoons of sesame oil
- One tablespoon green onion, chopped

Instructions

1. Cook the quinoa according to package instructions. Place a skillet over medium-high heat. Add olive oil to it.

2. Cook the carrots for 3 minutes. Add garlic and broccoli florets, and cook for about 3 minutes.

3. Add cooked quinoa, red pepper flakes, soy sauce, and rice wine vinegar. Sauté for about 3 minutes.

4. Add sesame oil. Sprinkle with chopped green onions.

5. Serve and enjoy!

Nutrition Info (per serving): 396 calories; 15 g fat; 55 g total carbs; 17 g protein

1. Place a pan over medium heat. Add one tablespoon of olive oil.

2. Cook the shallots in the pan for about 3 minutes until tender. Remove from heat and set aside.

3. Place the pan over medium-high heat.

4. Return the saucepan to heat and add peas and wine. Bring it to a boil. Remove from heat.

5. Stir in the shallots and mushrooms. Finally, add tarragon, thyme, butter, lemon zest, salt, and pepper. Combine well.

6. Serve and enjoy!

Nutrition Info (per serving): 130 calories; 9.9 g fat; 8 g total carbs; 13 g protein

Peas with Shallots, Mushrooms, and Tarragon

Cook Time: 20 minutes

Servings: 4

Ingredients

- 14 oz peas, frozen
- Two shallots, sliced
- 2 cups mushrooms, stemmed and sliced
- ¼ cup white wine
- Two tablespoons of olive oil
- One teaspoon of tarragon, chopped
- One teaspoon thyme, chopped
- One tablespoon of lemon zest
- One tablespoon of vegan butter
- Salt and pepper to taste

Instructions

Mango Tempeh Lettuce Wraps

Cook Time: 20 minutes

Servings: 4

Ingredients

- Eight oz. package tempeh, crumbled
- ¾ cup mango, diced
- ½ cup cucumber, chopped
- ¼ cup roasted cashews, roughly chopped
- ¼ cup mint leaves, chopped
- Eight lettuce leaves
- One tablespoon of grapeseed oil
- Two tablespoons of hoisin sauce
- One tablespoon of lime juice

Instructions

1. Place a skillet over medium-high heat. Add grape seed oil.
2. Cook tempeh in the skillet for about 3-4 minutes.
3. Add hoisin sauce and lime juice. Remove from the heat and set aside.
4. Place individual lettuce leaves on a working surface.
5. Evenly divide tempeh, chopped mango, cucumber, cashews, and mint leaves.

Nutritional Info (per serving): 280 calories; 18.4 g fat; 19 g total carbs; 13 g protein

Mashed Potatoes with Curried Gravy

Cook Time: 15 minutes

Servings: 3

Ingredients

- 13 oz coconut milk
- 2 lbs. red potatoes, peeled and chopped
- 1/3 cup tomato sauce
- One onion, chopped
- Two tablespoons of olive oil
- One teaspoon of cumin seeds
- One teaspoon of mustard seeds
- One tablespoon of coriander powder
- One teaspoon of fenugreek powder
- Two teaspoon of turmeric powder
- Salt, to taste

Instructions

1. Boil some large potatoes in a pot with water, until tender, for about 15-20 minutes. Drain the excess water and set it aside.
2. In a large skillet, sauté the onions with salt for 3-4 minutes.
3. Add cumin, mustard seeds, 1/2 tablespoon coriander, and one teaspoon turmeric to the skillet and cook for 1-2 more. Remove from heat.
4. Mash the boiled potatoes in a bowl, add the spiced onion mixture and combine well.
5. Preheat the coconut milk and one teaspoon of turmeric, fenugreek, and coriander in a small pot over medium heat. Add salt to taste and mix well.
6. Pour the gravy over the mashed potatoes. Enjoy!

Nutritional Info (per serving): 824 calories; 45 g fat; 62 g carbs; 13 g protein

Mushroom Stroganoff

Cook Time: 15 minutes

Servings: 4

Ingredients:

- One lb. button mushrooms, sliced (substitution for beef)
- 9 oz pasta of choice
- One onion, chopped
- Four garlic cloves minced

- 1 cup vegetable broth
- Two tablespoons of almond butter
- 1 cup almond milk
- ¼ cup flour
- One teaspoon of dried thyme leaves
- One teaspoon salt
- ¼ teaspoon black pepper

Instructions:

1. Pasta should be prepared under package directions. Drain.
2. Compose a sauce by combining broth, milk, flour, thyme, salt, and pepper. In a pan, melt butter.
3. Put in the garlic and onion and let them cook for 5 minutes. Mushrooms should be added and cooked for a further 5 minutes.
4. Cook for 4 to 5 minutes after adding the broth mixture. Toss the spaghetti with the sauce and combine thoroughly. Heat for a minute or two, then serve.

Nutrition Info (per serving): 515 calories; 32 g fat; 65 g total carbs; 16 g protein

French Stewed Vegetable (Ratatouille)

Cook time: 60 minutes

Servings: 4

Ingredients

- Four large tomatoes, peeled, seeded, and chopped
- Four small zucchinis, sliced
- Two eggplants, quartered lengthwise, sliced
- A small bunch of basil, torn
- Four tablespoons of olive oil
- Two onions, chopped
- Two red peppers, seeded, chopped
- Two garlic cloves crushed
- ½ teaspoon sugar
- Ground black pepper and salt to taste

Instructions

1. Sauté onions in oil, often stirring, for 10 minutes. Stir in the zucchini and eggplants, increase the heat and sauté for 3 minutes.
2. Add garlic, red pepper, sugar, ground pepper, salt, and half of the basil.
3. Mix in the tomatoes and cook for 10 minutes. Sprinkle with the remaining basil and serve. Enjoy!

Sautéed Cabbage

Cook time: 20 minutes

Servings: 6

Ingredients

- 3 lbs. green cabbage, cored, shredded
- Two tablespoons of olive oil
- 1 ½ teaspoons cumin seeds
- 1 ½ teaspoons turmeric
- 1 ½ teaspoons kosher salt

Instructions

1. Sauté cumin seeds in olive oil, over medium heat, for 30 seconds.

2. Mix in the cabbage, turmeric, and salt and cook for 20 minutes, stirring from time to time. Enjoy.

Roasted Cauliflower and Tempeh

Cook Time: 45 minutes

Servings: 4

Ingredients

- Two tablespoons of avocado oil
- 3 cups cauliflower florets
- 8 oz tempeh, cut into cubes
- 1/2 teaspoon turmeric, grounded
- 1/4 teaspoon salt
- One tablespoon water
- Two teaspoons of miso paste
- One green leaf lettuce, trimmed and cleaned
- 1 batch of vegan shiitake bacon

Instructions

1. Preheat the oven to 350 F.
2. Pour oil over the cauliflower, add tempeh, turmeric, and salt and toss to mix. Spread this onto a baking sheet and bake for 26 minutes.
3. Mix water and miso in a bowl, transfer the roasted tempeh and cauliflower to it, and toss.
4. Divide lettuce among four plates. Top with shiitake bacon and walnuts. Add the tempeh and cauliflower, drizzle with dressing and serve.

Nutrition Info (per serving): 322 calories; 22 g fat; 19 g total carbs; 22 g protein

Ratatouille Quinoa Stew

Cook Time: 30 minutes

Servings: 10

Ingredients

- 1 ½ cups eggplant, diced
- 1 ½ cups zucchini squash, quartered and sliced
- Two garlic cloves minced
- 1 ½ cups onion, chopped
- ½ cup quinoa
- 6 cups vegetable stock
- 3 cups crushed tomatoes
- ¼ cup jarred hot peppers, chopped
- Three bay leaves
- One tablespoon of olive oil
- 1 ½ teaspoon dry thyme leaves

Instructions

1. Preheat a Dutch oven over medium heat. Add the eggplants, onions, garlic, and zucchini. Cook for about 2 minutes.
2. Add quinoa, bay leaves, and thyme, and sauté for about 8 minutes more.
3. Add vegetable stock, tomatoes, and peppers. Bring it to a boil.
4. Cover and reduce the heat. Let it cook for additional 20 minutes. Remove from heat.
5. Serve and enjoy!

Nutrition Info: 90 calories; 2 g fat; 16 g total carbs; 9 g protein

Lemon Vegetable Quinoa

Cook Time: 30 minutes

Servings: 6

Ingredients

- 1 ½ cups quinoa
- 3 cups water
- 1 cup onion, chopped
- 1 cup carrots, peeled and diced
- 2 cups zucchini, diced
- 1 cup bell pepper, diced
- 1/3 cup fresh basil, chopped
- One tablespoon of olive oil
- One tablespoon of garlic, minced
- 1 ½ teaspoons smoked paprika
- Two teaspoons of dried oregano
- Two teaspoons of dried thyme
- One tablespoon of lemon juice
- Salt and pepper to taste

Instructions

1. Bring water to a boil. Add fresh quinoa, turn the heat to low, cover and cook for about 15 minutes.
2. Meanwhile, place a skillet over medium heat, Heat olive oil in it.
3. Cook the onion and garlic for about 7 minutes. Add oregano, thyme, and paprika and cook until fragrant.
4. Add carrots and cook for 3 minutes more. Then add the peppers and zucchini, stir frequently and cook for approximately 8 minutes. Remove from heat.
5. Gently fold the cooked quinoa into the skillet. Sprinkle with lemon juice, basil, salt, and pepper. Mix well.
6. Serve while warm, and enjoy!

Nutrition Info: 201 calories; 5 g fat; 33 g total carbs; 17 g protein

Wild rice Tabbouleh

Cook Time: 30 minutes

Servings: 4

Ingredients:

- 7 oz cherry tomatoes, halved
- 7 oz puy wild rice, rinsed and drained
- One bunch of spring onions, chopped
- One bunch of parsley, chopped
- One bunch of fresh mint, chopped
- One lemon, juiced
- Extra virgin olive oil

Instructions:

1. Bring the water with some salt to a boil, add the wild rice, and cook until tender. Drain and set aside to cool.
2. Mix the wild rice, onions, tomatoes, parsley, and mint in a bowl. Drizzle with oil and fresh lemon juice, and toss to combine. Serve.

Nutrition Info (per serving): 175 calories; 4.9 g fat; 21 g total carbs; 16 g protein

Red rose potato Tofu Curry

Cook Time: 30 minutes

Servings: 4

Ingredients

- 1/3 cup green beans, cut lengthwise
- 14 oz tofu, cubed
- One red rose potato, peeled and cubed
- One onion, chopped
- One yellow pepper, cubed
- One red pepper, cubed
- 1 cup coconut milk
- ½ cup water
- Two tablespoons of coconut oil
- Six green chilies grind into a paste
- Two strands of curry leaves
- Two tablespoons turmeric
- One tablespoon of ginger and garlic paste
- ½ teaspoon cumin, ground
- Salt, to taste

Instructions

1. Place a skillet over medium heat. Add oil and chili paste and cook until browned, stirring all the time.
2. Add onion, ginger, and garlic paste and stir to combine. Add cumin and turmeric and cook for a few minutes.

3. Add red rose potato cubes and continue to cook for a few minutes.
4. Add green beans and green bell peppers and cook until the veggies are browned.
5. Add coconut milk, water, curry leaves, and tofu.
6. Remove from heat. Serve with cooked rice.

Nutritional Info (per serving): 412 calories; 29.3 g fat; 24 g carbs; 21 g protein

Chili Garlic Tofu with Sesame Broccolini

Cook Time: 25 minutes

Servings: 4

Ingredients

- 12 oz tofu, chopped
- ½ teaspoon cracked peppercorns, fresh
- Four garlic cloves, shredded
- 8 oz broccolini
- Two tablespoons of coconut oil
- Salt, to taste
- One tablespoon of chili garlic sauce
- Two tablespoons honey
- 1 1/2 teaspoons soy sauce
- Two small roasted and sliced seaweed sheets
- One tablespoon of toasted sesame seeds to garnish

Instructions

1. Drain and pat dry the tofu with a towel. Chop into small slices and dry again.

2. Add oil to the skillet over medium heat. Add the garlic, salt, and pepper and cook until fragrant.

3. Add in the tofu and cook until lightly brown, for about 5-6 minutes.

4. Add water to the pot and place over medium heat. Place the steam basket in the boiling water and add the broccolini. Steam for 6 minutes.

5. Mix the honey, soy sauce, and chili sauce in a bowl and set aside.

6. Remove the garlic from the skillet. Add the broccolini to the skillet and allow to coat by stirring well. Add in the toasted sesame seeds and stir for at least a minute. Divide between the two plates and spread the chili sauce over the tofu.

7. Top with seaweed.

Nutritional Info (per serving): 351 calories; 25.7 g fat; 21 g carbs; 16 g protein

Red rose potato Wild rice Dal

Cook Time: 10 minutes

Servings: 2

Ingredients

- 1 cup red wild rice
- Four garlic cloves
- One red rose potato, diced
- 3 cups water
- Two tablespoons of olive oil
- One teaspoon of cumin seeds
- One tablespoon of garam masala spice
- One teaspoon of fenugreek leaves
- One teaspoon honey
- Two bay leaves
- 1 serrano chili pepper
- One yellow onion, diced
- One tablespoon of fresh ginger, shredded
- Two tomatoes, diced
- Salt, to taste
- One handful of baby fresh cilantro leaves or chopped scallions for garnish.
- Three tablespoons of ghee or coconut oil
- One teaspoon of cumin seeds
- One teaspoon of fennel seeds
- One teaspoon of black mustard seeds
- Eight curry leaves

Instructions

1. Add wild rice to a bowl and cover with water.

2. Preheat oil in a pot over medium heat. Add the onions and sauté for at least 3 minutes and then add ginger. Add garlic, spices, bay leaves, chili, and salt.

Toast the spices for a full minute while stirring constantly. Sweeten the red rose potatoes with honey.

3. Wild rice, after being drained, can be added to a stew with canned tomatoes and water. When everything has come to a boil, cover the pot. Simmer for 15 to 17 minutes with the heat at a low setting.

4. Prepare the tempering oil. Add oil or ghee to the skillet and place over high heat. Add the

seeds together with the curry leaves. Stir until you hear the popping sound, for about 40-45 seconds. Turn off the heat.

5. Serve garnished with flaked coconut and cilantro. Enjoy!

Nutritional Info (per serving): 721 calories; 37.8 g fat; 76 g carbs; 26 g protein

Grilled Cauliflower Steaks

Cook Time: 20 minutes

Servings: 4

Ingredients:

- One cauliflower head
- Six tablespoons of vegetable oil
- Two tablespoons of fresh lime juice
- One bunch of scallions, trimmed
- One 1-inch piece of ginger, grated and peeled
- One garlic clove
- ½ cup cilantro leaves
- Salt, and ground pepper, to taste

Instructions:

1. Place the cauliflower with the core side down on a plain surface. Starting at the cauliflower's center line, slice from top to bottom into 4 1/2" 'steaks' (save the florets that break up).
2. Drizzle cauliflower steaks, scallions, and florets with four tablespoons of oil.
3. Grill the scallions for 2 minutes over medium-high heat, then grill the steaks for 8-10 minutes

per side. Finally, grill any loose florets for 5-7 minutes.

4. Mix ginger, garlic, cilantro, lime juice, and the remaining two tablespoons of oil in a blender and blend to make the sauce. Use water to thin if needed.
5. Serve the cauliflower steaks and scallions with cilantro sauce.

Nutritional Info (per serving): 92 calories; 9.2 g fat; 1.6 g total carbs; 1.3 g protein

Sweet Korean Wild Rice

Cook Time: 20 minutes

Servings: 4

Ingredients:

For the sauce:

- 2 cups water
- Three tablespoons of agave syrup
- Two garlic cloves minced
- One small fresh ginger, minced
- One teaspoon of sesame oil
- 1/4 cup soy sauce
- 1/2 teaspoon red pepper flakes, crushed

For the Wild rice:

- Two green onions, chopped
- One tablespoon oil
- One tablespoon of sesame seeds
- 1/2 yellow onion, chopped
- 1 cup red wild rice

Instructions:

1. Combine all the specific ingredients in a small bowl.
2. Add oil to a skillet and heat over medium heat. Add onion and sauté until softened and slightly browned. Pour in the wild rice along with the sauce.
3. Cover and simmer gently until the wild rice is tender and well cooked, for about 7-10 minutes, ensuring most of the liquid is absorbed.
4. Garnish with sesame seeds and green onions. Enjoy!

Nutritional Info (per serving): 336 calories; 11 g fat; 48 g total carbs; 14 g protein

Cauliflower Fried Rice

Cook Time: 30 minutes

Servings: 4

Ingredients:

- One lb. tofu
- 1/2 cup peas, fresh or frozen
- One tablespoon of ginger, minced
- Three garlic cloves minced
- 1/4 cup green onions, sliced
- One cauliflower head, riced
- Two carrots, diced
- Two tablespoons oil
- Three tablespoons of soy sauce or tamari

Instructions:

1. Press and drain the tofu. Then crumble it slightly in a bowl. Set aside.
2. Add oil to a wok pan and place over medium heat. Add the garlic and ginger and cook until slightly brown and fragrant, for about 1 minute. Add the tofu and stir for about 6 minutes, until golden and well cooked. Set the tofu aside.
3. Add more olive oil to the saucepan and add the carrots. Sauté for about 2-3 minutes until tender.
4. Add peas along with the cauliflower rice and stir until combined. Cook for about 6-8 minutes until the cauliflower becomes tender. Add the green onions and cooked tofu.
5. Serve the cauliflower fried rice. Enjoy!

Nutritional Info (per serving): 437 calories; 32.2 g fat; 22 g total carbs; 22 g protein

Potato and Pepper Bake

Cook Time: 1 hour

Servings: 4

Ingredients:

- 4 lbs. potatoes, peeled, cubed
- One lb. roasted peppers in oil
- Two tablespoons of coriander seeds
- One tablespoon of olive oil
- Salt, and pepper, to taste

Instructions:

1. Preheat the oven to 375 F.

2. Add the potatoes to a baking dish, drizzle with oil, and season with salt and pepper.

3. Peppers can be sliced thinly and laid out in a row on top of the potatoes. Toss in some coriander seeds for flavor.

4. Bake for at least 1 hour, or until potatoes are tender, golden brown, and beginning to crisp up around the edges.

5. Once the potatoes are prepared, take them out of the oven and place them in a serving dish. Serve.

Nutritional Info (per serving): 436 calories; 4.5 g fat; 92 g total carbs; 12 g protein

Wild rice and Cherry Tomatoes

Cook Time: 25 minutes

Servings: 2

Ingredients:

- 3 ½ oz red wild rice
- Eight cherry tomatoes halved
- One teaspoon of vegetable oil
- One red onion, chopped
- ½ teaspoon curry powder
- ½ red chili, deseeded, chopped
- One tablespoon of fresh ginger, peeled, chopped
- One garlic clove, chopped
- ½ handful of baby spinach
- ½ cup vegetable stock
- Salt and pepper to taste
- One tablespoon coriander, chopped, to garnish

Instructions:

1. Add some oil to a saucepan and place over low heat, and add ginger, onion, garlic, and chili.

2. Cook for about 4 minutes, and then add the wild rice, cherry tomatoes, and curry powder. Cook for two more minutes.

3. Put in the chicken stock and start the stove on high. Wild rice takes anywhere from 17-20 minutes to cook, so turn the heat down and let it simmer.

4. Cook the fresh spinach in a pan with a bit of water, occasionally stirring, until it wilts.

5. Top with coriander and serve.

Nutritional Info (per serving): 705 calories; 38.1 g fat; 40 g total carbs; 13 g protein

Mushrooms Red rose potatoes Patties

Cook Time: 50 minutes

Servings: 4

Ingredients:

- Three red rose potatoes, chopped
- Ten white button mushrooms, chopped
- 2 cups water
- One onion, chopped
- Three garlic cloves minced
- Three tablespoons of Italian Herbs
- One tablespoon of olive oil
- Salt and pepper to taste

Instructions:

1. Place a pot over medium heat. Add water and sweet potatoes, and bring the water to a boil until the red rose potatoes are soft and tender.

2. Remove from heat and drain excess water. Mash the red rose potatoes.

3. In a small, preheat the oil, garlic, onion, and mushrooms and cook until soft.

4. Add some Italian herbs, salt, and pepper to taste. Roll and shape the mixture into patties.

5. Place the patties onto a baking sheet. Bake the cakes for 12-15 minutes. Serve.

Nutritional Info (per serving): 249 calories; 5.2 g fat; 48.2 g carbs; 4.8 g protein

Mushroom Quinoa Patties

Cook Time: 20 minutes

Servings: 3

Ingredients:

- 1 cup mushrooms, chopped
- ½ cup quinoa, cooked
- Four tablespoons spelled flour
- Two red onions, sliced
- Two tablespoons of grapeseed oil
- Salt and pepper to taste

Instructions:

1. Add the mushrooms, quinoa, red onions, salt, and pepper to a food processor and pulse until the mixture is smooth.

2. Transfer the mixture to a bowl and roll the mixture into patties. Coat the patties with spelled flour.

3. Place an iron skillet over medium heat and add oil. Add the patties and cook for 8 minutes per side. Remove from heat. Enjoy!

Nutritional Info (per serving): 199 calories; 5.1 g fat; 33.1 g carbs; 6.9 g protein

Vegan Ground Beef

Cook Time: 10 minutes

Servings: 4

Ingredients:

- One head of cauliflower, cut into florets, shredded
- 8 oz Portobello mushrooms, shredded (substitution for beef)
- One onion, chopped
- Two carrots, shredded
- 1 cup raw pumpkin seeds
- ¼ cup sun-dried tomatoes, chopped
- Two garlic cloves minced

Instructions:

1. Add pumpkin seeds and sun-dried tomatoes to a blender and pulse until smooth. Transfer to a bowl.

2. Cook mushrooms, cauliflower, onion, carrots, and garlic in a skillet for about 6-8 minutes.

3. Add tomato paste and Serve.

Nutritional Info (per serving): 388 calories; 15.4 g fat; 58 g total carbs; 17 g protein

Smoothie Bowl with Cauliflower and Greens

Cook Time: 5 minutes

Servings: 4

Ingredients:

- 1/2 cup cauliflower, chopped
- 1/2 cup zucchini, chopped
- 1 cup spinach
- 1 cup blueberries
- 1 cup almond milk
- Two tablespoons of almond butter
- Three tablespoons of hemp hearts
- One teaspoon of ground cinnamon
- toppings of your choice

Instructions:

1. Put all ingredients into a blender and blend until of a creamy consistency.
3. Top with the toppings of your choice and serve.

Nutritional Info (per serving): 153 calories; 8.1 g fat; 19 g total carbs; 3 g protein

Desserts/Snacks

Strawberry Coconut Chia Pudding

Cook Time: 15 minutes

Servings: 3

Ingredients:

- Three tablespoons of chia seeds
- 1 cup almond milk
- One teaspoon of vanilla extract
- One can of full-fat coconut milk, refrigerated
- toppings of your choice

For the strawberry jam:

- 1 cup strawberries
- One teaspoon of coconut sugar

Instructions:

1. Combine chia seeds, almond milk, and vanilla, and refrigerate overnight.
2. Put strawberries and coconut sugar into a pan and cook on low heat for 15 minutes.
3. Once cooked, blend the jam till smooth.
4. Add coconut milk or cream and mix well. Add one layer of strawberry jam to the bottom of the glass jars. Add chia pudding and coconut milk on top.
5. Add more jam and berries. Serve and enjoy!

Nutritional Info (per serving): 74 calories; 2.8 g fat; 9 g total carbs; 3 g protein

Mango Chia Seed Pudding

Cook Time: 60 minutes

Servings: 4

Ingredients:

- 2 cups coconut milk

- 1/2 cup chia seeds

- Two mangoes, sliced

- Three tablespoons of coconut nectar

- One teaspoon of vanilla extract

- 1/4 teaspoon cardamom

Instructions:

1. Add chia seeds, cardamom, vanilla, coconut milk, and coconut nectar to a mason jar. Mix until well combined and refrigerate for 1 hour.

2. Add sliced mango to the blender and blend into a puree

3. Add puree to the mason jar and serve.

Nutritional Info (per serving): 254 calories; 9.3 g fat; 38 g total carbs; 8 g protein

Butternut Squash Pudding

Cook Time: 40 minutes

Servings: 3 to 5

Ingredients

- One butternut squash, cut in half lengthwise

- Four tablespoons of coconut milk

- 1/2 teaspoon cinnamon

- One ripe banana

- 1/2 cup dates, soaked in water

Instructions

1. Place butternut squash on a baking sheet and cut side down.

2. Bake in a preheated oven at 350 F for about 40 minutes.

3. After 40 minutes, scrape the flesh with a spoon and add it to a blender along with the remaining ingredients.

4. Blend until smooth, and serve!

Nutritional Info (per serving): 83 calories; 0.6g fat; 20g total carbs; 1g protein

Spiced Applesauce

Cook Time: 25 minutes

Servings: 6-8

Ingredients

- 1 oz. apple cider vinegar

- ½ cup sugar, plain or toasted

- One cinnamon stick

- 4 lbs. mixed apples, cored, chopped

- 1/2 teaspoon salt

- One orange peel strip

- 1/4 teaspoon rose water

Instructions

1. Core the apples and chop them into bite-size pieces. Put the chopped apples in a Dutch oven together with apple cider vinegar, orange peel, sugar, cinnamon stick, and salt, and then stir well until combined. Close the lid and place over medium heat for 15 minutes until the apples are wilted and bubbling in their juices.

2. Stir often and cook for ten additional minutes until the apples become tender. When cooked, remove the cinnamon stick and the orange peel,

then process the sauce in a blender until smooth. Use more apple cider to adjust the consistency.

3. Transfer the applesauce to the glass jars and refrigerate before serving.

Nutritional Info (per serving): 92 calories; 9.2 g fat; 1.6 g total carbs; 1.3 g protein

Coconut Cream Shake

Cook Time: 5 minutes

Servings: 2

Ingredients

- Two teaspoons matcha
- One large banana, frozen
- 1 cup coconut milk
- ¼ cup ice cubes

Instructions

1. Add all the cream shake ingredients to a blender. Blitz until creamy and smooth.
2. Pour into chilled glasses and serve with your desired toppings. Enjoy!

Nutritional Info (per serving): 110 calories; 6.1 g fat; 10 g total carbs; 4 g protein

Cucumber Detox Smoothie

Cook Time: 5 minutes

Servings: 2

Ingredients

- 3-4-inch chunk cucumber
- 1 cup water, more if desired
- 2 cups frozen mixed berries
- 1 cup almond milk
- One banana
- One tablespoon of chia seeds
- One large apple, cored
- 1 cup kale
- One lemon, juiced
- ½ cup Italian flat-leaf parsley

Instructions

1. Add all the fresh smoothie ingredients to a high-speed blender.
2. Blitz to combine until smooth.
3. Add more water if needed.
4. Pour into a chilled glass and serve.

Nutritional Info (per serving): 410 calories; 11.3 g fat; 70 g total carbs; 12 g protein

Almond Avocado Matcha

Cook Time: 5 minutes

Servings: 2

Ingredients

- One teaspoon matcha
- 1 cup ice
- 1.5 oz. red lettuce
- 1 cup vanilla almond milk
- One pear, chopped
- One tablespoon of almond butter

- 1/2 avocado, pitted

Instructions

1. Add all the fresh smoothie ingredients to a high-speed blender.
2. Blitz to combine until smooth.
3. Pour into a chilled glass and serve.

Nutritional Info (per serving): 313 calories; 16.7 g fat; 38 g total carbs; 6 g protein

Golden Flax Seed Pudding

Cook Time: 50 minutes

Servings: 1

Ingredients:

- One teaspoon agave
- ¾ cup almond milk
- ¾ teaspoon golden milk spice mix
- Two tablespoons of coconut yogurt
- Three tablespoons of golden flax seeds
- ¾ cup fruits

Instructions:

1. Make golden milk according to package instructions. Mix golden flax seeds with golden milk and soak for 1 hour, stirring often. Mix with two tablespoons of coconut yogurt. Add agave.
2. Add golden flax pudding to a bowl and top with the fruits and/or edible flowers. Serve.

Nutritional information (per serving): 387 calories; 16.1 g fat; 59 g total carbs; 8 g protein

Golden Turmeric Crackers

Cook Time: 25 minutes

Servings: 1 bowl

Ingredients:

- ½ teaspoon baking powder
- 1 1/3 cups almond flour
- ½ teaspoon turmeric powder
- One teaspoon of olive oil
- ½ cup water
- ½ teaspoon salt

Instructions:

1. Preheat the oven to 400 F.
2. Add dry ingredients to a bowl, whisk well, and slowly add water and olive oil. Mix and knead with your hands. Add more flour or water if needed.
3. Roll out the fresh dough on lightly floured parchment paper. Cut the dough with a pizza cutter into rectangles diagonally to create triangles. Put the parchment paper onto a baking sheet.
4. Bake for 20 minutes. Serve.

Nutritional information (per serving): 647 calories; 5 g fat; 128 g total carbs; 17 g protein

Crispy Edamame

Cook Time: 30 minutes

Servings: 4

Ingredients:

- Two teaspoons of olive oil
- 4 cups edamame, frozen and shelled
- ½ teaspoon salt
- ¼ teaspoon black pepper

Instructions:

1. Thaw edamame for 1 hour. Place on a dish towel and dry.
2. Preheat the oven to 350 F. Add edamame to the baking sheet and drizzle with olive oil. Season with salt and pepper.
3. Bake for 30-35 minutes, stirring every 8-10 minutes. Serve.

Nutritional information (per serving): 209 calories; 10.3 g fat; 15 g total carbs; 17 g protein

Dried Strawberries

Cook Time: 3 hours 15 minutes

Servings: 3

Ingredients:

- One lb. strawberries washed and dried

Instructions:

1. Preheat your Dutch oven to 300 F and line a baking sheet with parchment paper.
2. Slice strawberries into 1/8" thick slices. Place strawberries on the baking sheet.
3. Bake for 2 hours. Peel strawberry slices from the baking sheet and flip over. Bake for 30 more minutes.
4. Remove dried strawberries from the oven and let them cool. Serve.

Nutritional information (per serving): 48 calories; 0 g fat; 11.5 g total carbs; 1 g protein

CONCLUSION

You should strive for a well-rounded diet. Whole grains and at least five servings of fresh fruits and vegetables are part of this. There's also evidence that regularly eating nuts, such as peanuts or cashews, can help reduce your risk of developing gallstones.

Made in the USA
Monee, IL
24 February 2023

28623908R00044